DATE DUE

GAYLORD   PRINTED IN U.S.A.

Period Make-up for the Stage STEP-BY-STEP

"The Ladies of St. James
They're painted to the eyes
Their white it stays forever
Their red it never dies
But Phyllida, my Phyllida!
Her colour comes and goes
It trembles to a lily
It wavers to a rose."

Henry Austin Dobson

Period Make-up for the Stage

STEP-BY-STEP

*How to create the authentic
looks of the past
– from Egyptian and Elizabethan,
to Restoration and Victorian,
to the 20th Century.*

Rosemarie Swinfield

Betterway Books • Cincinnati

First published in the USA in 1997 by
Betterway Books
F & W Publications, Inc.
1507 Dana Avenue, Cincinnati,
Ohio 45207, USA

© 1997 Text and charts Rosemarie Swinfield,
photographs A & C Black (Publishers) Limited

ISBN 1-55870-468-X

Originally published in 1997 by
A & C Black (Publishers) Limited
35 Bedford Row, London WC1R 4JH

A CIP catalog record for this book is available from
the Library of Congress.

Front cover photographs of Fritha Goodey
and David Oyelowo.
Back cover photographs of Rosemary Denny, Chris
Naylor, Hélène Corr and Ashley Hodgson.
Photographs taken by Colin Willoughby.
Photograph of Rosemarie Swinfield
by Steve Slayford.

Typeset in 11 on 12.5 pt Galliard
Printed and bound in Italy by L.E.G.O.

*To Cassie and James who
always believe in me
and Marian who made it all
work with her quiet assistance.*

Contents

Introduction

In my last book *Stage Make-up Step-by-Step* I covered the basic make-up techniques that everyone appearing on stage ought to know. I also included some period faces. This made me think about the make-up of the past and my thoughts were reinforced when I was asked to train someone in the fashion make-ups of the twentieth century. As I worked I realized that there has been a complete change of style every ten years since 1920. Of course it doesn't change overnight but you can see the new look developing at the end of each decade and then come to fruition in the early years of the next. Naturally there are always variations on each look and you see this particularly in the 1970s with groups like the Punks and their alternative image. Nevertheless there are always one or two looks that identify a decade and this book, for the first time, identifies these key make-ups for theatrical productions.

When we look back to past centuries the hair and make-up fashions are dictated by the Royal Courts of Europe, most particularly the French and English Courts. When I began my research I felt I knew quite a bit about this but I quickly learned that my knowledge was rather superficial. I discovered that like the paint of the Native Americans, African tribes and other indigenous peoples, the fashionable make-up of past centuries in Europe was also tribal; identifying and separating the powerful groups in society.

There are, for example, wonderful descriptions of the ladies of the French court in the late seventeenth century so coated in uniform make-up that it was difficult to tell them apart! I also discovered what I think is a quite astounding fact – from before the time of Queen Elizabeth I until the end of the 1920s most fashionable women in society wore white make-up. Why? Well, the whiter your complexion the better bred you were perceived to be and this was extremely important in terms of marriage prospects. Also white skin was sexually desirable so women passed recipes for whitening their faces and bodies from generation to generation.

Now we come to a problem because you rarely see this stark whiteness in portraits. Usually ladies of quality are painted with porcelain faces delicately flushed, never wearing the red and white paint which was the reality for centuries. It seems that the painters had an understanding with their wealthy patrons to show what they wanted to see and not the ravages of disease and the lead paint which ate away their skins. You also don't see the black patches which were used to hide the damage. But go to the diaries and literature of the past, look at the cruel cartoons lampooning society and you find the truth.

In theatre and sometimes in other mediums you don't often see accurate period make-up. The costumes will be right and

1960s Beatle and 1930s Hollywood Style

probably the wigs but where are the faces? Occasionally, as in plays set in the 1930s and 1940s, you see period mouths and lip shapes but so often the rest of the face for the period is missing.

This book is designed as a reference guide to the most important period looks. In each section you will find photographs, charts and a make-up routine along with a historical perspective and a guide to hairstyles, including facial hair for men. If a particular period is not included it either means that there is no strong look to discuss or that it is of little interest in production terms. Finally, you will see the word "paint" used extensively as you read. Until this century the term "make-up" was unheard of. I don't know who invented it, possibly Max Factor, I suspect, but it is very recent. Before it came into usage women, and sometimes men, "painted" their faces and make-up was known as paint.

I hope you enjoy the book, it shows the fascinating history of facial style, an art form open to us all.

Models

Before . . .

Here are pictures of all the models used in the book with either no make-up or their basic day make-up so you can appreciate the changes make-up can make to a face.

Look up the page references to find them in period make-up and costume.

David Oyelowo, pages 44, 98, 106

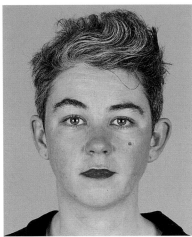

Hélène Corr, pages 53, 108

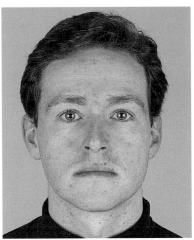

Stuart Murray, pages 77, 81, 84, 113

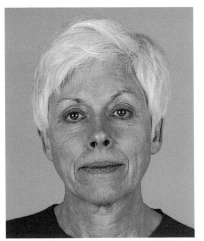

Rosemary Denny, pages 42, 86

Chris Naylor, pages 48, 59, 61, 91

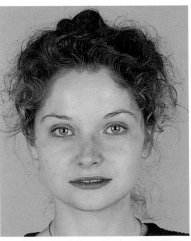

Fritha Goodey, pages 56, 78, 88, 100, 103

Sara Korsvnova, pages 50, 62, 74, 82, 95

Ashley Hodgson, pages 52, 68

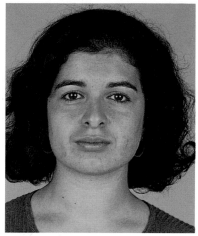

Zena Khan, page 92

Patricia Walters, page 46

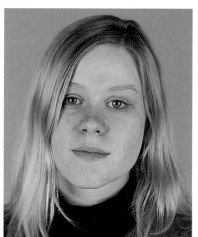

Kim Gladman, page 70

Victoria Gordon, page 18

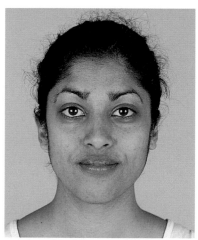

Priyanga Elangasinghe, page 110

Giles Fagan, pages 55, 64, 73, 97, 102, 105

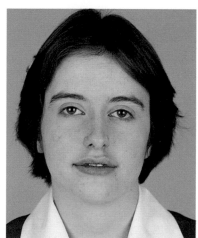

Alison Barker, page 65

11

Part One

Make-up Routines

It is helpful to understand how to apply cosmetics, and to know what goes on when. As a professional it is obvious to me, but I know from years of observation that it isn't always the same for you. For example, I couldn't count the number of times I have watched a student trying to apply a cream shader with a wet brush. It is the same with the make-up routine, remember that you must set everything that is creamy, with the exception of lipcolor, before you apply blushers, eyelines etc. or you will have problems.

Below is the order you should be using when you put your make-up on. For women I have given the option of cream eyeshadow before powder or powder eyeshadow after powdering.

Note: All the make-ups shown in the book are designed for medium size theatres. In smaller venues eyelines will not need extensions unless that is right for the period – for example the 1950s and 1960s. On large stages you will need to strengthen the extensions to make your eyes clear to the audience. This advice only applies to women!

WOMEN

1 Skin tonic
2 Foundation
3 Shading
4 Highlight
5 Cream eyeshadow
6 Powder
7 Powder eyeshadow
8 Top eyelines
9 Bottom eyelines
10 Socket shadows
11 Mascara
12 False Lashes – dependant on period
13 Eyebrows
14 Blusher
15 Lipstick
16 Body make-up

MEN

1 Skin tonic
2 Foundation
3 Shading – optional
4 Highlight (eyelids)
5 Powder
6 Rouge
7 Bottom eyelines
8 Mascara (optional)
9 Eyebrows
10 Lipcolor – dependant on period
11 Facial hair
12 Body make-up

Stage make-up

SKIN TONES

Women

In general, unless otherwise stated, Asian and Hispanic make-ups are covered in the basic routines. Black and darker skins are discussed separately.

Men

Since most of the male make-ups follow the basic routine, I have not separated skin tones unless indicated.

Basic Make-up

Women: Step-by-step

All actresses need to be able to present their faces on stage at their best. This requires a knowledge of shading and high-lighting to improve structure and the ability to make up your eyes to increase their size. Always remember that stage lighting is work-ing against you, changing the way the audi-ence perceives your face by emphasizing the pale areas. There is no such thing as a perfect bone structure but we all have the possibility, with the use of shading and highlighting, of achieving the best for our faces. The follow-ing make-up routine shows you the basic principles, but if you want to go into it more deeply I suggest you read my book *Stage Make-up Step-by-Step*.

Before you start, read the section on shading and highlighting on page 23.

Keynotes

- even foundation
- neutral eye make-up
- shading and highlighting for structure

Routine

1 Here is the model wearing no make-up. She has a pale, naturally broad face and the lighting is emphasizing that, making the face look both paler and wider. Before applying any make-up tone your skin with a skin freshener to suit the skin type.

2 Then apply a professional foundation evenly. These come as waterbased cakes, cremes, fluids and cream sticks – the choice is yours. Here I have used a television cream stick which gives a good cover. Apply it as warpaint first, in about five strokes, and then blend with a slightly damp sponge, adding more as required. The finished effect should be even with no redness showing but *not* heavy.

3 When the foundation is on, you then shade to improve your bone structure. Use a dark brown lining color which is easy to blend. Basic shading goes on the browbones, across the tip of the nose and under the

1

2 and 3

4   5   6

cheekbones. When the shading is finished you add the highlights. They are usually down the center of the nose, on the cheekbones and on the tired shadows under your eyes to hide them. Choose either a very pale cream or cream stick foundation. I have also used it to hide a few blemishes on the face. After this, powder well using translucent loose powder and a puff or cotton wool, *not* a brush.

4 For stage work a neutral eye make-up means adding eyelines, socket shadows, mascara and an eyeshadow that gives a sense of color without period or fashion. Brown eyeshadows are unsuitable because, on stage, they actually make the eyes appear smaller. Try, as here, a pale grey green or, for darker and Hispanic skins, a soft lilac tone. The eyeshadow should cover the whole eyelid from the edge of the lashes to the socket bone. Eyebrows frame the eyes and balance the bone structure. Adding mascara brightens and enlarges the eyes.

5 Dry rouge (blusher) used on the cheekbones and into the shading beneath them emphasizes good bone structure. This is the classic "made-up" position beloved by most actresses. However, it is incorrect for most period make-ups or if you want to appear unmade-up. When there is no particular period indicated in the production or you want to look made-up in a modern play but not "in fashion" this is the position to use.

Lipstick for any stage of reasonable size needs to be a clean soft red or peachy tone to read under the lights. Brown and plums on white skins tend to look both dark and flat, don't use them.

6 Here is the finished make-up. Notice the improvement in her bone structure and the skin texture. The eyes are now the focal point of the face as they should be. On stage she will appear to be wearing just a little make-up.

Before

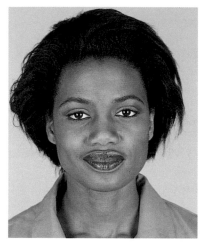

After

Routine: Darker Skins

Follow the routine as described but use foundation to match your skin tone. Apply lilac or bronze eyeshadow and black eyeliner and mascara. Use a darker shading and a yellow toned highlight. Apply deeper rouge and lipstick. These colors can be found in ranges like Flori Roberts.

Note: To make this an unmade-up look use highlight for eyeshadow, a soft lip color and the basic male rouge position.

Routine: Black Women

Before
Our model has a problem common to all dark skins on stage – natural shine which de-structures the face. Also she needs to balance the eyes and the mouth.
After
The finished make-up evens the skin tone and minimizes the shine. The eye make-up brings the emphasis back to the eyes.

Routine: Hispanic Women

Before
Here is our Hispanic model before make-up. She has a beautiful face with a squarish jaw and olive skin.
After
With make-up applied the skin tone looks more even, the face shape is more balanced and we can see the eyes clearly.

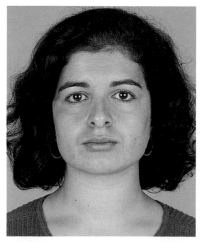

Before

After

Routine: Asian Women

You should follow the basic routine bearing in mind the advice given in the shading and highlighting section, page 23. However because Asian eyes have little eyelid showing here is a diagram to show you how to make the best of your eyes.

Eye detail: Asian women

Close-up eye make-up

The details of a classic stage eye make-up all play individual roles. Pale eyeshadow or high-light increases the lid size making the eye appear larger. Adding the top eyeline defines the edge of the top lid. The extension helps this for medium to large stages. It should look like an extended triangle at the outer corner. The bottom eyeline defines the lower lid, again increasing eye size, its extension is shorter than the top one and not a triangle. It does not go up into the inner or outer cor-ner of the eye as that would make the eye look small. The socket shadow defines the top of the eyelid and should be both more muted in tone and much wider than the eye-lines. Mascara thickens and lengthens the eyelashes completing the eye make-up. Apply all the steps in the correct order:

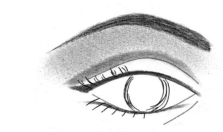

Eye detail: White, Hispanic

1 eyeshadow or highlight
2 top line
3 bottom line
4 socket shadow
5 mascara.

Note: It is really helpful to do one complete eye at a time. That way you can see if you are increasing your eye size. If it hasn't you have either drawn eyelines which are too heavy, brought them too close together at the corners or, horror of horrors, joined them up.

Eye detail: Black

Men:
Step-by-step

W hy, oh why are so many men lazy about make-up? Every actor needs to be able to apply a basic "straight" make-up to make himself look healthy under strong lighting. Lighting doesn't help your face, it actually works against it, making you look tired and unhealthy. Here is a simple routine shown on a white model. Darker skins should follow it bearing in mind the comments for their skin tone. Before you begin read the section on shading and highlighting on page 23.

Routine

1 Here is the model wearing no make-up. The skin looks uneven, pale and shiny.

2 The simplest foundation to use is a light wash of cake make-up. You apply it with a wet sponge in strokes like warpaint and then quickly blend before the water evaporates. You can then add more as necessary with a

drier sponge. The cake sets itself and can be used on body skin as well.

3 To make your eyes appear larger highlight your eyelids with a very pale cream stick or lining color (not white!). Blend the highlight where you can feel the eyeball under the skin and right down to your eyelash roots.

1

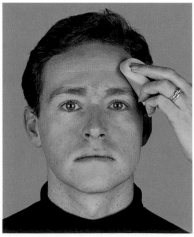

2

3

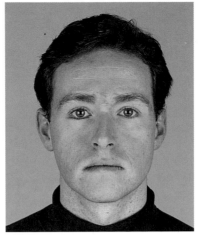

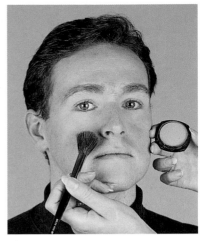

4

5

6

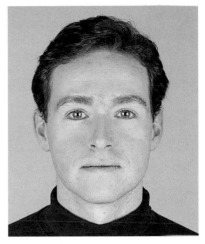

7

4 Powder will set the highlight and any other moist areas. Use loose translucent powder and press it carefully over the make-up with a puff or cotton wool. Keep going until the powder completely disappears.

5 On all but little stages it is enormously helpful to use a simple underline to increase the size of your eyes. Draw it with a well sharpened pencil or cake liner and keep the line thin. You can see how the effect makes the eye look bigger in the photo. Add a little cake mascara to darken your eyelashes if they are fair and strengthen the eyebrows with pencil or cake if they need emphasis.

6 Lighting can drain your face of color even with a foundation applied. A little dry rouge or blusher gives a healthy natural look if you apply it like this and in this position.

7 Here is the finished make-up, it simply makes the face healthier looking and empha-sizes the eyes in a low key way. It doesn't challenge your integrity as an actor!

Eye detail

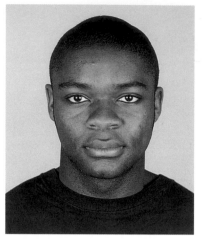

Before　　　　　*After*

Routine: Darker Skins

Here is the same make-up routine as applied to a black actor. Once the skin tone is darker than a tan you need to match foundation to your own skin color. If, as is the case with our model, you have a really dark and even natural color you may not need a foundation but you should use powder to reduce the natural shine of dark skins. Use a more yellow toned highlight for the eyelids, eye lines and eyebrows will be black. Surprisingly a deep toned blusher can be helpful as it breaks up the uniform darkness of the face.

Eye detail

Detail: Asian eye

22

Shading and Highlighting

These techniques are used to improve or alter your bone structure. Shading makes areas of your face less noticeable under the lighting and to do this you use a cream lining color in a dark brown. Highlighting emphasizes areas of the face, making them more noticeable under the lighting – for this you use very pale cream or cream stick foundation. Always apply an even amount of foundation before using these techniques or the result will look patchy.

Begin with the shading, using a brush for precision, and then blend carefully with your fingertips. Then apply the highlight working in the same way. When you have finished, powder to set the make-up making sure that you don't rub the shadow and highlights into each other.

For white skins I used a dark brown Supracolor to shade and a television face cream stick IW to highlight.

If you have dark skin you will need a really dark brown liner to shade, perhaps even black. The Kryolan company do one called SF1 in their Supracolor range. To highlight on deeper skins you need a yellow toned highlight. I used one called GG in this book.

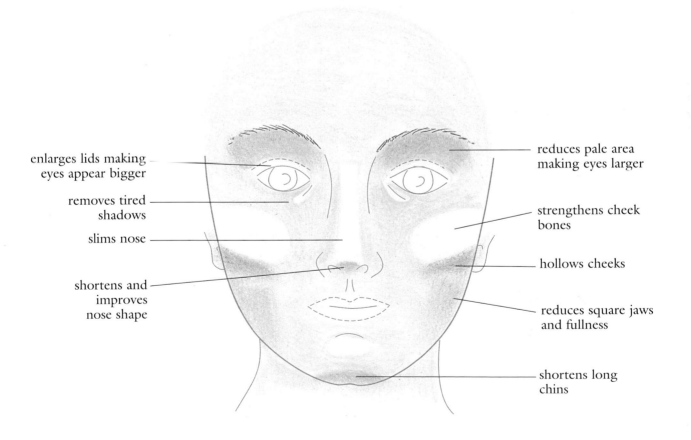

enlarges lids making eyes appear bigger

removes tired shadows

slims nose

shortens and improves nose shape

reduces pale area making eyes larger

strengthens cheek bones

hollows cheeks

reduces square jaws and fullness

shortens long chins

Techniques and Special Effects

Beards and Moustaches

A period beard or moustache can be reproduced in several ways. Originally actors used crepe wool, pressing it flat or "laying" it on to the face in thin glued layers, a similar technique using real hair is used in the film business. But unless you are experienced I wouldn't advise it as the results could be hilarious. Good, and poor, glue-on beards and moustaches are widely available.

The best, knotted on fine hair lace, are expensive but worth it. I have used several in this book. Simple, narrow moustaches, however, can be drawn on using cake eyeliner or a sharp, good quality, eyebrow pencil. This works well for small shapes but don't attempt anything larger, unless it is supposed to be a joke.

Simple drawn on moustache and beard

To make this Charles II moustache and lip beard delicate strokes of dark brown cake eyeliner were drawn in the position that the hair would grow naturally in.

Here is the same technique used to reproduce a typical 1930s narrow moustache. If you choose to use pencil, which is waxy, remember to powder afterwards to avoid smudging.

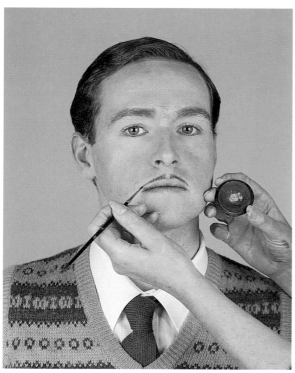

Drawn on moustache

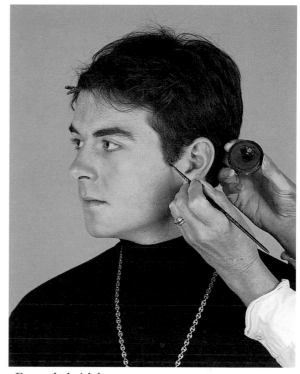

Extended sideburns

Sometimes natural sideburns are not quite long or thick enough. They can be supplemented by lengthening or filling in the gaps with pencil or cake liner

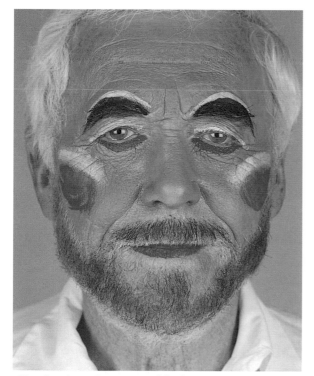

Darkening the natural hair

Sometimes an actor grows a beard or moustache and it comes out either gingery or grey. If you want to darken the facial hair to match your own or a wig the easiest way is to brush cake mascara through it in the correct shade. Use a toothbrush rather than the silly little brushes sold with mascaras today. Here I have used dark brown to reduce the whiteness of the beard and moustache. You need to wet the brush to apply the mascara.

HOW TO APPLY A FALSE MOUSTACHE SECURELY

Routine

1 Prepare the area by patting skin tonic on the skin.

2 Paint a layer of spirit gum on to the skin and let it dry completely. (This will act as a shield against perspiration which can loosen the moustache.)

3 Paint another layer of gum on to the skin and press the moustache on to it, positioning it carefully.

4 Press the edges down with a velour powder puff – this will make the edge of the hair lace disappear.

5 Smile to check that you haven't glued over your smile lines by mistake!

BEARDS

Unless you have a sweaty chin you will not need the first layer of spirit gum so, follow the routine, leaving out step (2), being careful to center the beard on your chin.

Note: If you are using a fake beard or moustache for a long run it is better to buy medicated spirit gum – your skin will bless you! Always remove the gum with a proper spirit gum remover.

OPPOSITE: *Natural moustache and beard, darkened*

A Victorian moustache

Edwardian beard and moustache

Putting on a Hair Lace Wig

Set wigs with hair lace fronts need careful handling. Always place them on your head from the front and remove by lifting off from the back. Never try to change the style yourself, the wig dresser uses special pins and setting spray and if you have no experience of wig dressing you could find yourself with a disaster literally on your hands.

Routine

1 Long hair will need wrapping round your head and securing or put into pin curls. Cover your own hair with a stocking top or one of the special nets sold for this purpose. If the wig is heavy, secure the stocking with bobbypins above your ears.

2 Carefully remove the wig from the block (it will be held there with long pins) and with one hand at the front and one at the back position it on to your forehead and pull it gently back over your head. With a thin brush handle tuck in any stray hairs which may have escaped from the stocking.

3 The hair lace will now need gluing down or the light on stage will reveal the edge to the audience which can be very distracting. If the wig is correctly positioned there should be two little hair lace flaps just above your ears, if not your wig is on crooked. Put a little dab of spirit gum under each flap and press the hair lace on to it stretching it downwards as you do.

4 Hold in position until the spirit gum dries. Check the lace edge across your forehead and if it is still a little frilly place tiny dabs of spirit gum at intervals under it. Press the edge down with a velour puff or soft dry sponge.

Never:
- cut the lace back – the wig supplier will kill you!
- put make-up over the lace – it shows it up beautifully, especially after a few performances.

Some hair lace is heavier than others like the one on the wig here but at a reasonable distance it completely disappears so don't worry.

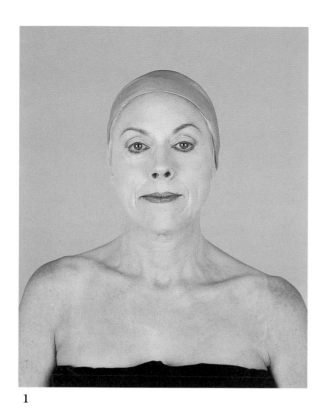

1

2

3

4

29

How to make a French Pleat

The hair styles on page 92 and page 100 are created using a French pleat. Any time you have to add a small hairpiece to your hair it is really useful to put the hair into a pleat before pinning the hairpiece on. Here is the way to do this.

You will need:
- a tail comb and a brush
- bobbypins and hairpins (large and small)
- hairspray
- some large metal clips

1 It is easier to do this if the hair is not freshly washed and soft. Unless you have thick hair, tease your hair before you begin, to give it more body. A tail comb is the best implement for this.

2 Separate the front section of your hair and brush it forward. Smooth the side of your hair back and slightly upwards, spray and secure with metal clips. Sweep one side across the back of your head and hold in place down the center with a line of bobby-pins. Spray well.

3 Fold the other side across your hand into a vertical roll and pin it along the edge and in behind the bobbypins. Use big hairpins to secure the pleat and smaller ones to tidy away any stray hairs into the shape. Spray well. Carefully brush the front hair back and secure with fine pins. Spray again and remove metal clips.

4 Here is the finished style. To give it a little more height, take the point of your tail comb, slide it under the front section of your hair and carefully lift. This must be done after securing and spraying the hair.

Note
- the best hairspray for this is a firm hold one
- a top knot hairpiece is just pinned at the top of the pleat as shown in the photograph on left

1

2

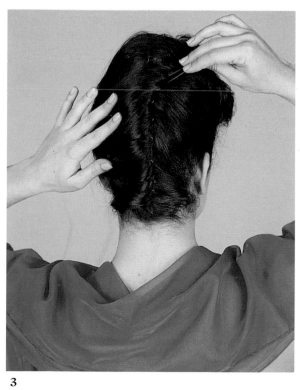

3

4

Blocking Eyebrows

To create the look described on pages 56 and 59 you need to block out the eyebrows. The old fashioned way of doing this is to rub a thin piece of wet soap through your eyebrows and then press them flat. The disadvantage can be that as the soap dries the hair can spring out. There is a product called Eyebrow Plastic which works in a similar way but I prefer the following technique.

Be sure to do this *before* applying the foundation. It is always tricky to hide anything but thinnish eyebrows if you are close to the audience or on camera but it works very well for medium to large stages.

You will need:
- spirit gum
- mortician's wax
- Sealor or liquid latex
- a clay modeling tool with a flat end
- a toothbrush

Important: Do one eyebrow at a time or you will have trouble with the spirit gum.

Routine

1 Quickly work spirit gum through the eyebrow and brush it up hard with the toothbrush to flatten it against your forehead. Do the other eyebrow and check that there are no loose hairs.

2 Dig out a piece of wax and smooth it on to the back of your other hand. Smear a thin amount of wax over your eyebrows. The aim is not to completely cover them but to fill in the gaps between the hairs and provide a key to hold the foundation later. Use too much and you will look deformed!

3 Smooth Sealor or latex over the wax. I use my finger because both products can clog up brushes but you may find a brush easier. When the seal is dry apply your foundation – cream stick gives the best cover on blocked out brows.

To remove the wax and spirit gum you will need to use a proper spirit gum remover available from all theatrical make-up stockists.

Sometimes it is necessary to only block out the end of the eyebrows as you will see in the 1930s section, on page 78. To do this, follow the routine, but only glue flat the outer half of each eyebrow and then cover them as described above.

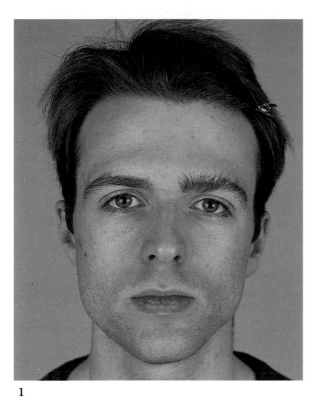

1

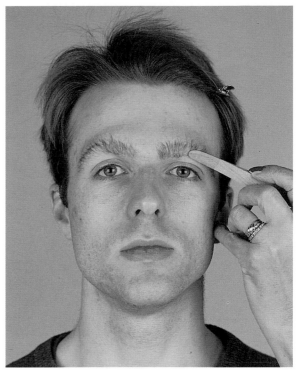

2

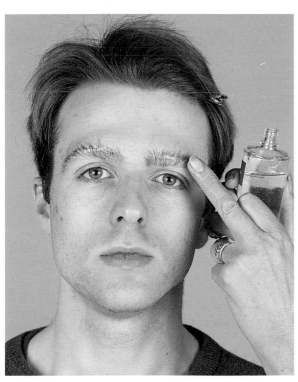

3

*"Their faces are besmeared
and pierced
With several sorts of patches
As if some cats their skins had flead
With scars, half moons and notches."*
Sir John Mennis

Patches

There are records of face patching from the time of Elizabeth I. At the Court black velvet or taffeta patches were applied to the temples to relieve headaches. In the early seventeenth century clergymen condemned them as instruments of the devil but, by the end of the century, they, along with most fashionable men and women, were wearing them. Patches were sold by pedlars with other cosmetics.

After their initial use as a remedy they became popular for hiding pock marks and the ravages of white lead paint. Originally circular in shape they began to appear as stars, half moons, hearts and lozenges. At the court of Louis XIV a whole language of "les mouches" appeared, similar to that of the fan. Patches in different places meant different things; at the corner of the eye passion,

the center of the cheek gayness, on the upper lip kisses, the side of the nose sauciness, l'assassin on the forehead was majestic and so on. A heart worn on the left cheek indicated that a lady was engaged and unavailable. By 1700 patching had reached its zenith with descriptions of Duchesses wearing fifty patches. They had also grown elaborately; trees containing two turtle doves, coaches and eight horses and other absurdities were popular. As well as velvet, satin and taffeta black patches, some women wore paper ones, and red leather was used too. The fashionable carried them in elaborate little boxes and applied them with gum arabic or mastic.

Later they had political connotations with eighteenth century Whig ladies patching on one side of their faces while Tories patched the other.

Jacobean

Restoration

18th Century

Cuts and Scars

In this section you will find two simple techniques for wounds which look extremely realistic even when you are nose to nose with your audience. Apply foundation before using them. On bare skin powder before you begin.

TECHNIQUE 1 – COLLODION SCARS

You will need:
- a bottle of rigid collodion
- highlight
- powder
- jelly blood

Important: Collodion is a liquid which contracts the skin. Never use it close to your eyes, on sensitive skin or areas of broken veins. To achieve maximum effect it needs to be used on the loose parts of the face or neck, it gives little result on firm areas.

As well as giving excellent scar effects, collodion is also good for strangulation marks.

Routine

1 Paint a line of collodion with the brush provided. Remember sword or knife cuts are thin at the ends but wide in the center. Allow five minutes for the collodion to dry, you will feel it pulling. If you don't see a noticeable effect you probably need to change the position to a softer area.

2 Using a brush apply a broad area of highlight to the skin on each side of the scar - blend to soften the paleness slightly. If you want an old scar effect you should now color the collodion with either a soft amount of brown red (pale skins) or a very dark brown or black (black skins).

If you have a pale skin and are creating a bleeding scar color the collodion with a strong amount of brown red liner – Kryolan EF9 Supracolor is excellent for this.

3 Whatever your choice, powder the scar and the surrounding area.

4 Add jelly blood. Why jelly blood? Well it doesn't dry out and on black skins it catches the light especially well. If you want blood really running, then you will need to use liquid blood.

1

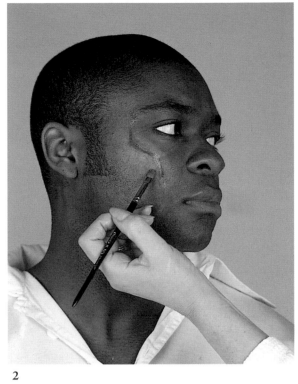

2

3

4

TECHNIQUE 2 – TISSUE SCARS

Facial tissues are a really cheap way of creating realistic scars, they can also be used for scabs. Don't attempt to make big effects with them, it doesn't work.

You will need:

- pink or white tissues
- spirit gum
- red brown or very dark brown lining color

Routine

1 *Pale skins* – stipple a small amount of red brown over the area you have chosen.

Black skins – do the same using dark brown or black depending on your skin tone.

2 Powder

3 Divide a tissue and carefully tear off a small jagged shape (don't use scissors!) to fit into the center of the coloring leaving plenty showing around the tissue. Paint a thin amount of spirit gum on to the skin and press the tissue over it (at this point you can ruin the effect by either folding the tissue or using too much gum which will saturate it.) Allow the spirit gum to dry completely.

4 Depending on your skin tone, color over the tissue area using a brush with either the red or a darker liner. As you paint be careful to leave little areas of the pale tissue showing to give the wound texture. If you don't it will look flat and unrealistic.

Then take a little of your chosen color and increase the "reddening" round the wound.

5 Here is the finished result.

Optional Extras

- you can add "pinpricks" of blood to the finished wound
- powder used over the tissue will give a dry old scab effect

Removal

Use spirit gum remover or surgical spirit.

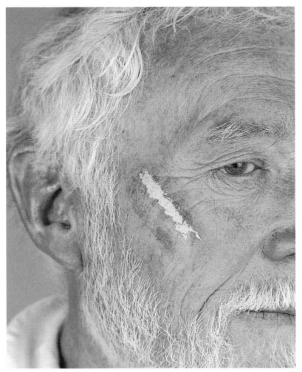

Step 3

Step 4

Step 5

Part Two

The Make-ups

The Ancient Egyptians

*"For her own person -
it beggared all description"*
Enobarbus on Cleopatra,
Antony and Cleopatra

ANCIENT EGYPTIAN WOMEN

In Ancient Egypt both sexes wore highly stylized make-up and wigs. Cosmetics were professionally produced and packaged. Yellow tinted foundations were favored by men and women, although some men used an orange tint. The liquid foundation was made from powdered ochre and other pigments and was applied to the face, arms and chest. Eyebrows were shaved and redrawn in an exaggerated shape using kohl. This was also used for lining eyes and was available in black and colors. Although using kohl made

a fashion statement, it also protected eyes against dust. Eyeshadow was widely used, often with one color for the top lids and another under the eyes. For example, Cleopatra used blue black above her eyes but Nile green underneath them. The colors might be changed according to the time of day. Lips and cheeks were rouged and henna was used on the soles of the feet, palms of the hands and as an ancient form of nail color. Like the later seventeenth century Restoration beauties, women traced in the

Eye close-up

Side view

42

Eye detail

Instead try an Aquacolor or face paint which will look matte and painted.

6 Trace in eyebrows and eyelines lightly with a brown pencil. When the shapes are right, color over with a really sharp black pencil or liquid liner.

7 Paint a different color in a band along under the bottom eyeline.

8 Mascara.

9 Apply matte orange tone rouge along cheekbones.

10 Color lips with orange or red lipstick.

Optional

• color nails, palms of hands and edges of feet with orange body paint.

Routine: Black, Darker Skins

Follow above routine but use your own foundation color. Eyeshadow – greens or copper would work well. Use a deeper rusty rouge tone. Lipstick should be a dark orange red.

veins on their breasts with blue dye and the really fashion conscious actually gilded their nipples!

Keynotes

• extended black eyebrows and eyelines
• green, turquoise or terracotta eyeshadow
• exaggerated black wigs

Routine

1 Apply yellow tan foundation very evenly to all areas of exposed skin. Alternatively use a yellow foundation for a really authentic look.

2 Shade to give high cheekbones and a slim nose.

3 Highlight cheekbones and center of nose. Highlight tired shadows.

4 Powder well. The skin should look matte.

5 Apply eyeshadow color to top lid and up to eyebrows. Don't use powder shadow, it will not have enough strength of color.

Eye detail: Black, Darker Skins

ANCIENT EGYPTIAN MEN

In Ancient Egypt it was commonplace for men as well as women to use make-up regularly; they also used perfumed oils and unguents. When they died these cosmetics went with them into the tomb in preparation for their journey into the next world. Both men and women used a yellow paint on their faces and bodies but only men wore orange. This foundation paint came as ground pigment and was kept in highly decorative boxes and jars. All men, from Kings like Tutankharmen downwards, lined and colored their eyelids with kohl. It was kept in tubes, often several linked together, and applied by slaves with saliva and a small stick. This early make-up was made by priests and sold for profit, but later on it was produced commercially. Soap being unheard of, bodies were cooled and at the same time perfumed, by solid cones of oil balanced on the elaborate wigs of the period.

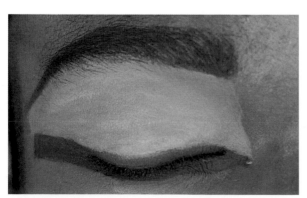

Eye close-up

Side view

Keynotes

- yellow or orange skin tone
- stylized and elongated eyelines and eyebrows
- colored eyelids
- elaborate black wigs or headdresses

Routine: White, Hispanic, Asian

1 Use yellow tan cake make-up or creamy cake. For really exaggerated characters use an orange tone. Apply it on face, ears, neck, arms and chests. If the rest of your body looks pale and can be seen, apply a normal light tan base.

2 If your character is handsome or elegant and your face is naturally heavy or broad, shade under your cheekbones and across the end of your nose (see shading and highlighting, page 23).

3 Highlight down the center of the nose and over your cheekbones.

4 Powder.

5 Apply bright green or terracotta face paint or Aquacolor over eyelids extending it outwards at outer corners.

Note: Use a brush and just a little water to apply color. Stick your chin up and look down your nose in a mirror to get at your eyelids. Do one at a time and allow it to dry to avoid smudging.

6 Powder eyelids.

Eye detail

7 Draw a black thickish line around the eyes and extend it out at the corners. A sharp pencil is the easiest way to do this. Add a line of another color underneath.

8 Use a black pencil to draw eyebrows.

9 Rouge is optional, use as in female make-up on page 43.

10 Same for lips – I suggest a little red rubbed over them.

Eye detail: Black, Darker Skins

Routine: Black, Darker Skins

Use no base or one to match your skin tone, otherwise follow the routine above.

The Elizabethans

ELIZABETHAN WOMEN

When Elizabeth I became Queen, she gave the lead in the use of prominent make-up, wearing the fashionable red and white paint of the period. Although this was often lead based, clearly she used one of the alternatives, otherwise she would have died, as many women did, from lead poisoning. Sadly in attempting to keep the years at bay her make-up became increasingly grotesque as she grew old and her eyesight became dim. Her ladies sometimes rouged the end of her nose and as Elizabeth had barred mirrors from the palaces she didn't see the cruel joke.

Most of the ladies of the court followed Elizabeth's lead, as did some men. Egg white was painted over the white base to glaze it, cheeks were rouged with ochre pigment or mercuric sulphide. Lips were colored with cochineal mixed with gum arabic or egg white. This make-up was commercially produced for the Court. During this period patches began to be worn, made from taffeta or velvet, to ward off headaches. Red hair, in imitation of the Queen's wig, was fashionable. Some women powdered their hair with gold too.

Keynotes

- white skin
- heavily rouged cheeks and lips
- bright red hair
- plucked eyebrows

Optional

- high forehead – often shaved

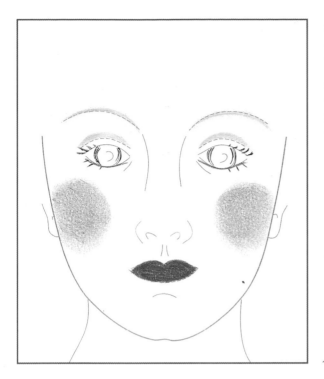

fatten the face. To emphasize the top eyelids, shade along the edge of socket bones. Shade to slim the nose.

4 The only highlighting you will need is on the eyelids. Surprising, you can use your foundation to highlight them *if* you apply the cream stick with a brush, doing that gives a greater intensity of color.

5 Powder well, preferably using a white matte loose powder.

6 For the young Queen draw on high, thin arched eyebrows using a red brown pencil. For the older Elizabeth use dark brown. You can also just ignore the eyebrows.

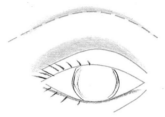

Eye detail

Routine: White, Hispanic, Asian

This routine is based on the Queen's make-up but for other Court ladies you would do a softened version of it.

1 Unless your eyebrows are very fair or thin you may need to block them out before starting this make-up. See Special Techniques, page 32. If your hairline is quite low you could also block some of that out too.

2 The face should look completely coated in whiteness. Bearing in mind that lighting makes foundation appear paler, I suggest that for the young Queen and attractive ladies of the Court you use a cream stick make-up in the palest skin tone available, e.g. Kryolan 1W Paint stick, which will look white but not grotesque. For the older Queen white would be better, e.g. Bob Kelly white Cremestick. You will need a stick make-up to give the "painted" look and to cover any blocked out areas efficiently.

3 The fashionable face shape of the period is oval so that square jaws will need shading, as will fuller faces. Remember pale foundations

7 The eyes should look quite bald and heavy lidded so the only lining should be soft brown underlines plus a socket shadow.

8 To keep the bald look to the eyes mascara with cake mascara rather than roll-on which would make the lashes too important.

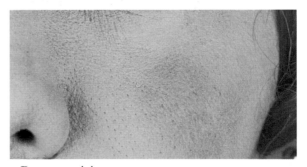

Rouge position

9 Using an orangey tone in a matte dry rouge apply the color to the sides of the face and cheeks - be generous with the older Queen!

10 Paint the lips bright red keeping the shape fairly round and small.

Female eye: Black, Darker Skins

Routine: Black, Darker Skins

I used a darker model for the photograph and was just able to use a white base on her but only do this yourself if your skin is quite pale, otherwise it will look grey. Instead apply your usual foundation but powder heavily. Follow the advice for shading and highlighting adjusting according to your own face shape. Obviously you will use black pencil for your eyebrows and lower eyelines. Your rouge will need to be a strong red to give the desired effect and if you have full lips just color them as usual using a red tone.

ELIZABETHAN MEN

The Elizabethan gallant was a very elegant creature indeed with his perfumed gloves, doublet and silken hose and lace edged han-kerchief. His clothes were richly decorated, he changed his cloak three times daily and he wore a stiff ruff holding his head high in an attitude of disdain. Although a man of action, at court he primped and prinned like any lady of fashion. Perfumed, painted, his hair curled and his beard dyed auburn as a compliment to the Queen, he carried a small steel mirror in his hat brim to check his appearance. Younger gentlemen, like minaturist Nicholas Hilliard, wore their hair framing their faces in an abundance of curls, sometimes with one long lock tied with a ribbon. Their neat beards were pointed and they sported moustaches with either long ends or a slight upturn. They rouged and some men whitened their faces like the court ladies; it was customary to wear one dangling

earring. Older men wore their hair straight and behind their ears and their beards were longer.

Keynotes

- rouged cheeks
- curly hair or wig
- pointed small beard and moustache

Routine

For all but the most dandified young gallants this is a basic make-up with a rouge position change and added facial hair. You will need a warm toned rouge color, the position is along the cheekbones from just about below the middle of the eye to the hairline at the sides of your face. Suck your cheeks in to find your bones. Serious dandies would be white faced like the Queen. Refer to the Fop on page 59 for information on this. Obviously those with dark skins wouldn't try this.

Older courtiers would have just a basic make-up.

Most men would have a beard and moustache as in the photograph.

Facial hair detail

The Early 17th Century

The Jacobeans

> *"A lome wall and painted
> face are one;
> For th' beauty of them
> both is quickly gone."*
> Arthur Dowton

JACOBEAN WOMEN

With the accession of James I to the English throne the use of make-up became more discreet. Among the clergy and moralists it was equated with the works of the Devil! Nevertheless women of all classes painted using white, flesh colored and pink lead based paints. The paint usually stopped at the chin making a curious contrast with the skin of the neck. Many women also used white powders. Moist rouge was used with paint and dry rouge with the powdered faces. They sometimes used blue, grey or brown eyeshadows and fair browed ladies were known to darken their eyebrows. Lips were sometimes rouged with a rosy red moist rouge. Hair was worn flat on top but with extravagant curls at the sides of the faces. Some patches were worn but less extensively in England than in other parts of Europe, however, the fashion was growing.

Because of the gory nature of many Jacobean plays, I have included a section on cuts and scars, see page 36.

Keynotes

• pale skin and rosy cheeks
• patches
• heavy lidded eyes

Routine

1 I think that for our purposes the face should not be as white as in Elizabethan times, but it should be pale with perhaps a pinky tone. Make-up was discreetly applied in this period. If you have a good skin, you could use a fluid foundation which gives good cover, otherwise choose a theatre base like a cream stick or Aquacolor.

5 Powder lavishly to give a matte effect.

6 Line the eyes as for your straight make-up and add a socket shadow.

7 Mascara, and for very pretty ladies, use a pair of subtle false lashes. Color your eyebrows naturally.

8 Lips are often described as cherry red in this time so use red with a touch of blue: apply to the whole of the lips in a softly rounded shape.

9 Rosy cheeks were in vogue. Smile and apply a pinky rouge to the fatness of your cheeks.

10 Patches are optional, but they became particularly fashionable later in the century.

Mouth detail with patch

2 Full faces were fashionable but if your face is naturally plump shade under your cheekbones to give some structure. You can also shade to improve your nose shape.

3 Highlight away tired shadows, although in these tragic plays perhaps they should be left! Highlight the center of your nose if it needs more structure.

4 Although eyeshadow was available I think it should be reserved for characters like whores in plays of this period. Instead of eyeshadow use highlight to enlarge your eyelids – try white (well blended) with very pale faces.

Routine: Black, Darker Skins

Follow the routine using the colors recommended for straight make-up but change the lip and rouge tones to something a little bluer.

Eye detail

Eye detail: Black, Darker Skins

JACOBEAN MEN

Following the accession of James I to the English throne there was religious persecution which led to the Gunpowder Plot and the departure of Puritan dissenters for the new lands of America. In 1607 an intrepid band of men and women landed and established a village they named Jamestown in honor of the King who had persecuted them. The Spanish influence on fashion established in the second half of the sixteenth century continued. The Elizabethan large ruffs became smaller and the invention of starch, denounced as vanity by the Puritans, meant that they were no longer supported by a wire frame. Eventually ruffs became "falling collars" trimmed with lace.

Men of Fashion wore their hair as long as they could and those who couldn't wore wigs. Men generally grew beards. In an early portrait the king wears a moustache with curled up ends and a squared goatee beard,

but other men wore fuller beards and down-turned moustaches. Some men still painted their faces but it was not the norm.

Routine

Basically for this period all you will require is your straight make-up. Make-up on men was considered to be effeminate so when they painted it was very discreet. Those who dared to wear it used rouge on their cheeks, flesh tone powders and occasionally a little lip color. A very few men did apply beauty spots. Hair was worn long and loose with small beards and neat moustaches.

If your character needs a cut or scar, see page 36 for routine.

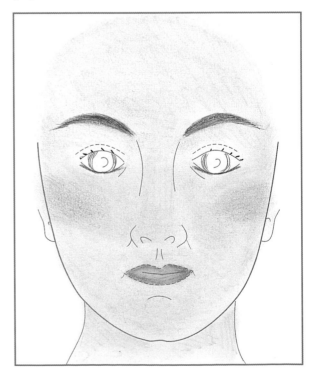

The 17th Century

The Restoration

RESTORATION WOMEN

"My wife seemed very pretty today, it being the first time I had given her leave to wear a black patch."

Samuel Pepys, 1660

The plays of this period are still very much part of the repetoires of English and French theatre today. At the dawn of the seventeenth century, despite all the efforts of the clergy, make-up had become very much part of the toilette of fashionable women. But with the restoration of Charles II to the English throne, after the restrictions of the Puritans, face painting reached new heights of extravagance.

Charles brought with him the fashions of the glittering court of Louis XIV at Versailles. Upper class women used ceruse, a white or pink paint, although others preferred to powder with white lead or borax. These dangerous substances actually destroyed their complexions, necessitating more and more to be applied to hide the damage. Old women painted heavily to hide their wrinkles and the paint often cracked and fell off. It was also, of course, poisoning them and they knew it. From the beginning of the century blue, brown and grey eye make-up was available and ladies darkened their eyebrows. Everyone rouged heavily. Hair was worn flat on top with little curls round the hairline and side ringlets; fashionable hair colors were black and brown. But the most important element of this make-up was the use of patches. Made from taffeta or silk all women of quality wore them. In France a whole language of "Les Mouches" evolved and great ladies wore as many as eight at a time and carried more in little boxes. In the American Colonies, however, few women used cosmetics.

Keynotes

- white skin
- bright circles of rouge
- patches
- hair flat on top with side ringlets

be translucent. For a white lead flat effect use unscented white talc.

6 Rouge was used extravagantly to give glowing cheeks. Choose a soft red, coral or bright pink. Apply as in diagram.

7 Prominent eyes with big lids were the height of fashion. To achieve this you will need a socket shadow in soft brown to emphasize your top lid. Fade it carefully along the edge of the socket bone following the shape of your eyelid. Draw a soft faded eyeline along the top lid and the roots of your lower lashes.

8 Mascara and add a pair of subtle fake lashes.

9 Eyebrows should be well trimmed and thinnish. Arch them softly for pretty ladies and for more extreme characters draw high, thin, black brows.

10 Full lips were the height of fashion – the most popular color used was cherry red as here.

11 Use a matching water based or liquid body make-up to cover your neck, blending it down to your cleavage.

12 Paint on or apply the patches. It is actually easier to draw them on using black pencil, cake or liquid eyeliner. If you want to stick them on choose simple shapes like circles or hearts and glue them with spirit gum or eyelash adhesive. See page 34 for further information.

A heart on the left cheek indicated that the wearer was engaged or unavailable. After marriage it would be changed to the right cheek.

Routine

1 For extreme characters use a white cream stick foundation. For elegant ladies I suggest a very pale color, like Kryolan IW which will look white but not clownlike.

2 The fashionable face of this period was full and double chins were desirable. I think we can forget the chins but otherwise unless your face is naturally full don't shade.

3 Highlighting is only necessary if you look tired and the pale base has not hidden the shadows. Use your base tone on a brush to cover the tiredness.

4 Some fashionable women wore eyeshadow. Brown and grey will look too modern to us, so a medium blue will be a better choice. For women, like our model, who didn't wear eyeshadow use highlight instead.

5 Powder heavily. Ceruse had a curious sheen so if you wish to reproduce, to a degree, that effect your powder will need to

Eye detail with eyeshadow

Eye detail: Black, Darker Skinned women

Routine: Black, Darker Skins

Follow routine but use your own foundation. Blue eyeshadow will, I think, look wrong, I suggest a lilac tone would look more period for deeper skins. A deep rosy red will give the right look for lips and cheeks.

RESTORATION MEN

"To Whitehall, to the Duke (of York), where first he put on a Periwig today: but methought his hair cut short in order thereto did look very pretty of itself, before he put on his periwig."

Samuel Pepys, 1663

When Charles II was restored to the English throne he brought with him the fashions of the French court, among them some of the oddest male garments. These included petticoat breeches, with their linings hanging down, which were tied with bows above the knee. These were worn with loose shirts hanging out. Everything was festooned with bunches of ribbons. One suit and cloak of the time is described as trimmed with 36 yards of silver ribbon, and a pair of petticoat breeches with 250 yards of ribbons tied in bunches.

Later on the King adopted Eastern costume swearing never to return to French fashion. During Charles' reign the long hair of the cavaliers was replaced by the periwig – long, curly, full bottomed, very heavy wigs – Charles' was black. Because of the weight and size of the wigs some men, like soldiers, wore smaller "campaign" wigs. For comfort most men either cut their own hair short or shaved their heads. To protect their heads from the cold at night, night caps were commonplace for men. During this period some gentlemen wore small moustaches and some were clean shaven. Small lip beards - a little tuft of hair under the center of the bottom lip - were also fashionable. At one time or another the King sported all of them. Older men continued to wear the neat pointed beard and moustache of the court of Charles I.

Routine

This is a basic make-up with an added small moustache and, as here, a lip beard. The moustache and beard in the photograph are drawn on (see page 24) but if you are close to your audience the beard in particular will need to be made with crepe or real hair.

The 18th Century

The French Court and its Influence

LADY OF FASHION

French Court fashion continued to be a major influence on English high society until the French Revolution. The use of toxic paints remained, causing the death of many famous beauties. In the American colonies supplies of ceruse, Spanish wool, hair powders and other cosmetics were available to a limited degree.

Now the fashionable face shape was oval with a high forehead which meant that many women had to find ways of hair removal. Faces remained white with exaggerated arched eyebrows. The cheeks were rouged even more generously and looked aflame with color. Smaller lip shapes became the mode. Patching continued unabated and at the French court it was often difficult to tell the ladies apart – they looked so uniform in their make-up.

> *"A young gentlewoman of about nineteen years of age (bred in the family of a Person of Quality lately deceased) who paints the finest flesh-colour wants a place."*
> advertisement in
> *The Spectator*, 1711

Hair was dressed up until eventually it reached ludicrous proportions making it impossible for women to sit upright in their carriages. These towering styles were styled over wooden or iron cages, padded out with crepe wool and held in place with bear grease. Feathers, ribbon, jewels and even models of galleons in full sail decorated these monstrous concoctions. The styles stayed in for months and were heavily powdered with white or other colored leads and often became infested with vermin.

Keynotes

- white face
- high, thin, black eyebrows
- lots of bright rouge
- patches
- powdered wigs and hairstyles

Routine

1 Unless your eyebrows are fair they will need blocking out completely before you start. See page 32.

2 Apply a dense white foundation being careful to cover the eyebrow area well.

3 Powder heavily.

4 Carefully trace in high, arched eyebrows. These are always tricky to match, so, try dotting the shape on at first and then draw in a fine black line. Foolish, elderly ladies should have one brow a little different from the other for effect. Calculating, hard women characters look good with the arch drawn a little outwards.

Eye detail, most women

Eye detail, hard woman

5 Since we are not using eyeshadow here you will, for a medium to large stage, need fine top and bottom eyelines with subtle extensions and a socket shadow.

6 Mascara top lashes only and add false eyelashes for medium to large stages. They are unnecessary for small theatres or in the round productions.

7 Apply rouge in glowing red to the side of the cheeks blending it into the hair line.

Lips

8 Color your lips with scarlet in a small rose-bud shape.

9 Apply make-up to your neck and chest to match your face and add a touch of rouge to the fullness of your breasts.

10 Add patches to the face, collar bones or the high point of your décolletage.

Eye detail: Black, Darker Skins

Routine: Black, Darker Skins

Follow the routine using a foundation to match your own skin and a bright rouge and lipcolor. If your mouth is large it would be a mistake to try to make it appear smaller so just make the shape rounder.

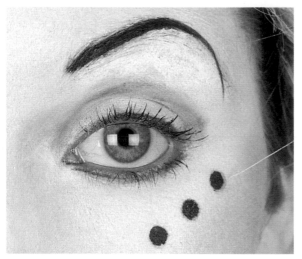

Close-up of eye with patches

18th Century Men

At the beginning of the 1700s a man wearing noticeable make-up would have been considered effeminate but by the turn of the century all gentlemen of fashion were noticeably painted. Older men followed the fashion in the hope of looking younger and the plays of the period are full of foolish, over made-up, old husbands being cuckolded by pretty young wives.

Elegant gentlemen rouged their cheeks and lips and wore a patch or two (see pages 34). But the more extreme fops went much further, emulating the elaborate ladies of fashion. They whitened their faces, shaved their eyebrows and redrew them in high black arches and heavily rouged their cheek-bones and mouths. Their patches were more showy and like the ladies of the court they carried patch boxes.

Many gentlemen shaved their heads to wear the wigs of the period which changed from the full bottomed periwigs of the Restoration to the powdered and tied wigs of the 1800s. However, there appears to be no record of colonial men wearing make-up during this period.

THE FOP

"A pretty fellow lacquers his pale face with as many varnishes as a fine lady."
The Connoisseur, 1754

Keynotes

- noticeably whitened faces
- high arched eyebrows
- rouged cheeks and lips
- patches

Routine

1 Block out eyebrows (see page 32) unless very fair.

2 Apply white or very pale cream stick foundation with a slightly damp sponge. The finish should look coated with make-up but not thick.

3 With a brush paint pale blue eyeshadow from the eyelashes right up to your eyebrows, finishing at the top of them in an arched shape.

4 Powder well, and carefully, with white or translucent loose powder. Check by running your fingertips over the whole face to make sure there are no sticky bits.

Eye detail

5 Lightly trace on the new arched eyebrow shapes with a brown pencil and when they match, powder them and go over the shapes with a black pencil. If it goes wrong paint foundation over the problem area and re-powder.

6 Draw a soft brown line along the roots of your lower lashes to emphasize your eyes. Add a little mascara.

7 Using a brush or cotton wool apply a circle of bright red or orange red dry rouge to the center of your cheeks. Silly old duffers would wear much more rouge and apply it badly.

8 Really foppish men painted their lips with rouge. A bright red lipstick will create the right effect. Make the shape smaller than your own mouth.

9 Add patches – a crescent moon with star looks good and could be combined with other shapes.

Lips and patches

Routine: Black, Darker Skins

Don't attempt to use a white base, you will simply look grey. Instead concentrate on the other details. Use a lilac eyeshadow rather than blue, and black eyebrows, lines and mascara. To show up on dark skin your range will need to be deeper in color as will your lipstick. Look in ranges like Flori Roberts which have the right colors.

GENTLEMAN OF FASHION

Routine

1 Apply a straight base in a healthy color.

2 If you need to look very glamorous shade under your cheekbones and across the end of your nose (see page 23).

3 Highlight your eyelids for medium to large stages.

4 Powder the face carefully.

5 Apply a fine dark brown line along the roots of your lower eyelashes and if they are fair add a little mascara.

6 Gentlemen of fashion should have elegant eyebrows so brush yours up with a tooth-brush and then brush the ends downwards. You can then pencil in a slight arch to give a quizzical air. Don't attempt this if you have very big eyebrows, it could look silly.

7 Using a rusty tone dry rouge on a large brush, color along your cheekbones. If you overdo it powder over the problem, it will soften the color.

8 With a black pencil place a beauty spot on your cheek or just above the corner of your mouth in an elegant position.

Optional

Lipstick is optional, only use it if your own lips are rather pale.

Routine: Black, Darker Skins

Follow the routine remembering that you will need a brighter rouge and black for eyebrows, eyelines and mascara.

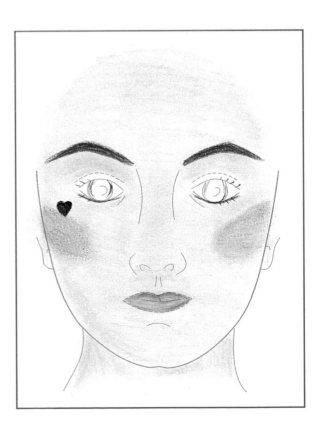

The 19th Century

The Victorians

VICTORIAN WOMEN

Even before the start of Queen Victoria's long reign there was a noticeable move away from the extremes of the eighteenth century. The French Revolution and the rise of Napoleon lead to much softer, almost ethereal fashions worn with hair softly curled and shaped back from the face and for a time rouge went out of fashion. In England, although some older women clung to their paint make-up, under the influence of a moral monarchy, became socially unacceptable. It didn't disappear but it became very subtle. Wives rouged, and powdered to a milky paleness discreetly, and husbands assumed their complexions were their own.

By the mid-century, however, Parisians were again wearing noticeable make-up and some courageous Englishwomen followed suit. Many poor women wore crude bright yellow wigs, daubed their faces with flour, charcoaled their brows and lashes and red-

dened their lips and cheeks. They, of course, would have been totally unacceptable in polite society. The American Colonies followed England's lead although Arnold J. Cooley comments on their passion for whitening their necks with carbonate of magnesia. Despite censure a vast array of different types of rouge was available and many fashionable women tinted the veins on their faces and chests and shaded their cleavages for evening wear.

Keynotes

- pale, milky skin
- soft pinky rouge
- natural eyebrows
- center parted hair looped back over the ears and into a chignon or worn with soft side ringlets.

Routine: White, Hispanic, Asian

1 The skin needs to look pink and white. If you are naturally olive skinned use the palest

foundation which will work well on you without your skin looking "dead." I would suggest perhaps two shades lighter than usual.

2 Shade and highlight to improve your facial structure as necessary for your character.

3 Powder to give a velvety smoothness for fashionable society ladies and more naturally for other women.

4 Apply a cream colored powder highlight to the eyelids to give natural looking big lids.

Eye detail

5 Line your eyes using dark brown for those with brown to fair hair and black only if your own hair or a wig is black as well. For a small stage you will not need a top eyeline.

6 With a matte powder shadow in dark brown, give yourself a soft socket shadow. Again, if you already have large eyelids, this will be unnecessary on a small stage. Brush through your eyebrows and color if necessary.

7 Mascara to give naturally dark eyelashes.

8 Smile and apply matte pink rouge to the fatness of your cheeks. Blend the edges carefully with your finger tips. For a totally natural color I suggest using a cream rouge, applying it earlier, before powdering.

9 Color your lips naturally with lipstick that matches and slightly heightens your own lip color.

10 Apply make-up to your body skin to match your face. Victorian women prided themselves on their milky skins and worked hard to achieve them, often using tinted liquid make-up.

11 Optional – trace in the veins on your breasts with blue pencil.

Rouge detail

Routine: Black, Darker Skins

Follow the routine using colors appropriate to your skin tone. Use just a little salve on the lips to give a slight sheen.

Eye detail

63

The walrus moustache

VICTORIAN MEN

"For my part I prefer the shows of life's winter to the best made peruke, and even a bald head to an inferior wig."

Habits of Good Society, 1859

Keynotes

Beginning of century
- short hair brushed forward on to the clean shaven face.

Reign of Victoria
- hair parted and brushed downwards – length mid-ear to just below the ears
- side whiskers sometimes worn without a moustache, often growing very low down the face
- moustaches - generally of the walrus type

Routine

This is a straight make-up with added facial hair. Do your face first before gluing on the facial hair. Make sure that the area where the hair is to be added is well powdered before you begin. See page 26 for instructions.

By the beginning of the century only a few dandies, fops and elderly gentlemen trying to look younger, still wore noticeable make-up and with the dawning of the Victorian Age it was frowned upon. Nevertheless George Washington was among American gentlemen who both powdered and wore perfume. Hair fashion changed suddenly from the wigs of the 1780s to the natural hair styles of the early 1800s. You can see the influence of Napoleon Bonaparte in the short hair style combed forward which was favored by the Prince of Wales and other gentlemen. But gradually the fashion for side whiskers developed along with side and center partings. By 1855 Prince Albert was sporting full side whiskers, a side parting and a walrus moustache. Macassar oil was so popular as a hairdressing that it was necessary to use anti-macassars to protect chair backs from staining. Not everyone wore this style, artists like Oscar Wilde and Aubrey Beardsley rejected the fashion and wore short hair with no side whiskers or moustaches.

The Kaiser moustache was popular with Victorian and Edwardian men

Victorian and Edwardian

Theatrical Make-up

THEATRICAL MAKE-UP – WOMEN

The first lighting developed especially for the theatre was Limelight but this was quickly replaced by footlights. Originally candles and then electric, this reflected light took both colors and structure from actors' faces and so they resorted to strong make-up to counter it. It looks very odd to us today but in the circumstances worked surprisingly well.

Proper theatrical make-up was created by a Victorian opera singer, a German named Ludwig Leichner. Before he developed theatre make-up actors used a combination of the paint and powder that you have read about in previous sections of this book, combining it with things like burnt cork to darken their eyebrows and faces and Indian ink for age lines. As well as the damage it caused

their skins and the potential threat to their lives there was another problem – when they became hot on stage the make-up ran down their faces.

Frustrated by these problems Leichner approached the chemistry faculty of Wurtenburg University with an idea for something better and they produced a grease formula for him which he, and his wife, made up for members of the Opera Company. They made grease sticks, fat ones in skin tones and thin ones in primary colors for eyes, lips, cheeks and aging. It was revolutionary and became so popular that by the end of the century he had founded the Leichner Company and greasepaint was born. It is still available today.

Despite the fact that women had been

permitted to appear in public on stage since the 1700s there is very little written advice for them in early make-up manuals. The wonderfully named Harefoot and Rouge who wrote the earliest book of advice barely mention us! Women were supposed to know what to do. From what there is available this is the routine.

Routine

1 You could be totally authentic and use greasepaint as your foundation. If so, bear in mind that your skin should look very, very pale. You need to use No. 1 greasepaint foundation. To apply it put a little cold cream into the palm of your hands and mix the greasepaint stick into it, then apply the mix to your face with your fingers and blend. Alternatively, use a base like cream stick in a really pale shade applying it heavily.

Eye close-up

2 There is no advice for shading to slim the face but I am sure clever actresses realized that a brown under their cheekbones improved their face shapes so I added a little to the model in the photograph.

3 The popular eyeshadow was blue. You will need to use a strong blue which could be a grease stick or a lining color - powder shadow will not do. Blend it over your eyelids.

4 Paint a line of white greasepaint or lining color under your eyes, following the eye shape.

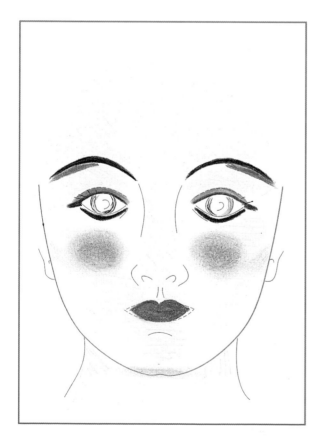

Eye detail

5 Paint a line of bright red greasepaint, lining color, or if the worse comes to the worse, lipstick, under your eyebrows working from the center to the outer ends.

Warning – red lipstick is very pigmented and may stain your skin for a day or two.

6 Smear a little red on your finger and apply it to the "apple" of your cheek (smile to find this). Because you are working on top of an unpowdered base you may find that you need to add more. The rouge should look bright.

7 Blend a little of the red across the point of your chin.

8 Powder. Actresses of the period would have used white powder so to recreate this you could use baby powder. Be careful not to rub or the colors will smear together. Keep powdering until all the baby powder is absorbed. You can, of course, use your usual translucent powder but this is more fun!

9 Using a black pencil define your eyebrows and draw a line along the top eyelids extending out and slightly downwards at the outer corners. It should look like two little black sticks. Draw another line under the white line beneath your eyes.

10 Mascara didn't exist at this time but actresses melted black greasepaint and using a matchstick applied little "beads" of it to their eyelashes. You could use a thick black mascara.

The make-up lit by footlights

Here is the finished make-up lit by the authentic lighting of the period.

Routine: Black, Darker Skins

Apply your own foundation heavily then follow the routine using the colors as given above.

The mouth

11 Color your mouth bright red in a rounded shape.

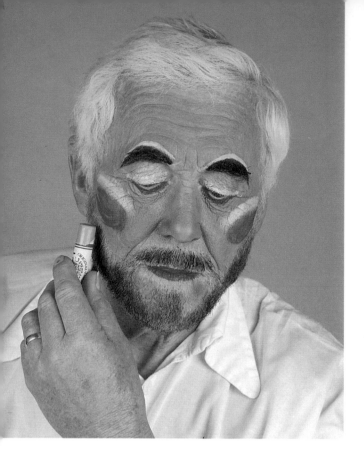

Routine

1 You need a fairly bright foundation. The greasepaint mix would be numbers 5 and 9. Otherwise use a base with an orangey tone.

2 Using a white greasepaint or cream stick, paint your eyelids.

3 Paint white above your eyebrows and on the high points of your cheekbones.

4 Using a red lining color or cream rouge, paint a line under your eyes and under the center of your eyebrows.

Eye detail

THEATRICAL MAKE-UP – MEN

Footlights forced actors to use dramatic make-up just so their faces could be seen across the blast of cold white light. Although the make-up seems crude it worked. Indeed some of the best compares well with the great make-up of later actors like Sir Laurence Olivier. In particular Sir Henry Irving's techniques were way ahead of his time. Here is the basic routine for a straight male make-up. It should be done with cream or grease foundation to achieve an authentic effect.

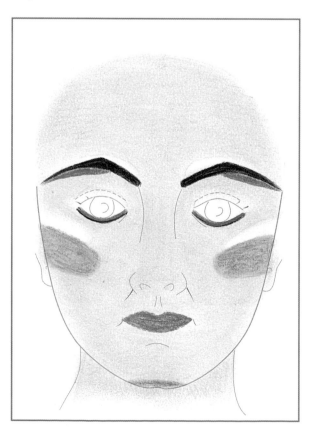

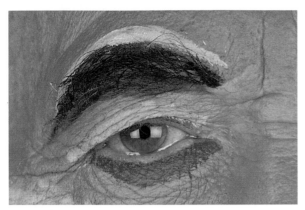

Eye close-up

The make-up lit by footlights

5 Take a little red and blend it with your fingertips along your cheekbones under the white, finishing at the hair line. Blend some across the point of your chin.

6 Powder carefully using translucent powder or baby powder. It is easy with grease or cream to smear things together so you need to be careful.

7 With a black pencil draw a strong eyebrow shape - eyebrows are heavily emphasized in these make-ups.

8 Fill in your mouth shape with red.

Here is the finished make-up lit by the authentic lighting of the period.

Optional

For larger stages apply a black eyeline beneath the red under the eye as in the chart.

Routine: Black, Darker Skins

Follow the routine using the same colors but use your own foundation color applied heavily.

The Late 1800s to 1910

The Edwardians

EDWARDIAN WOMEN

Although Edward VII did not become king until 1901, his glittering court at Marlborough House greatly influenced society. His beautiful wife Alexandra's hairstyles and clothes were widely copied. For women of means this was the last period, coming before the Great War in 1914, when they could spend serious time – and a great deal of money – on how they dressed. Exquisite gowns were a status symbol and all women dressed as well as they could possibly afford. Obvious make-up, although seen in Paris, was still frowned on in England and America. Queen Alexandra, however, enameled her face to a perfect paleness but, it is said, only in the evening. Conversely, the use of powder and rouge was acceptable in America only in the daytime. In 1902 Helena Rubenstein opened her first salon in Australia and Maybelline launched petroleum jelly for eyelashes.

Society ladies were the great icons of the period, their images sold on picture postcards. Their long hair was worn initially back and dressed in elaborate coils down the back of the head with a mass of tight little curls at the front and later folded over rats (sausages of crepe or horsehair) into the high, full pompadour's style of the famous Gibson girls. Most fashionable women wore powder and rouge discreetly and working girls rouged to look healthy.

Keynotes

- pale skin
- natural eyebrows
- soft rouge
- hair up, coiled at the back with lots of front curls
- hair padded with false pieces and swept back into a high chignon

Routine

Many women were still enameling so:

1 Your skin should look very pale and matte so use a foundation with good cover.

2 Shade and highlight as suitable for your character, see page 23 on shading and highlighting.

3 No respectable woman wore eye make-up in this period so just highlight your eyelids to make them larger. If you are playing a tart then use bright blue shadow and take it right up to your eyebrows. See separate section on page 65 for actresses theatrical make-up of the period.

4 Powder to give a matte, even texture. Translucent powder is fine but for prostitutes I would suggest white powder or talcum powder.

5 Depending on your theatre size, line your eyes as in the straight make-up section and mascara.

6 Eyebrows were generally left in their natural state although from the photographs of the period some women were plucking them. Poor street women would have penciled brows.

Eye detail

The mouth

71

7 Elegant women used subtle rouges which were available as powders, pomades, liquids and papiers poudre - little rouge impregnated papers. To achieve the look brush a matte pinky or peachy tone dry rouge to the center of the cheeks in a large soft circular shape.

8 The most desirable lip color, according to a beauty book of the period, was that of red strawberries. However, this was supposed to be achieved naturally - for example by biting the lips or rubbing them with vinegar. A soft rosy red lip color rubbed on with your finger would achieve the same effect but you may prefer to use a lipbrush in which case block your lips well after applying it.

Eye detail: Black, Darker Skins

Routine: Black, Darker Skins

Using your normal colors follow the above advice deepening the lip and cheek colors to show up delicately against your skin tone.

EDWARDIAN MEN

> *"The apparel oft proclaims the man."*
> Hamlet

In marked contrast to the extravagance of female fashion, Edwardian men appear quite plain. Their outfits became both sober and uniform with class deliniated by the cut and quality of the clothes. Individualism was expressed by shirts, ties, cravats and the occasional exotic note like Oscar Wilde's green carnation. Edward, Prince of Wales and later King, was an important influence on London Society where there was an outfit for every part of the day as well as activities like shooting, golf and the new fangled tricycling. Although the Prince's set was considered racy, no gentleman within it would have crossed his legs when sitting in the presence of ladies, in that more formal society it would have been too intimate a gesture.

During this period hair became shorter, usually with a side parting, and was worn brushed back from the forehead. Otherwise all men sported moustaches and, following the King's example, many grew Vandyke beards. Others favored waxed moustaches without beards like those of Napoleon III and Kaiser Wilhelm II whose version with upturned ends spawned many copies of the "Kaiser Moustache". Some older men clung to the mutton chops so popular with the Victorians and even youngish men like W.G. Grace, the cricketer, and playwright George Bernard Shaw grew full, long beards.

Keynotes

- hair to ear length, side parting and brushed naturally back
- full moustaches with longish ends *or* waxed extensions either going straight out at the sides or twirled upwards. Moustache wax is available from theatrical stockists
- Vandyke beards – this is like a large goatee extending up to the ears

Routine

The make-up is a basic straight stage make-up with added facial hair. See page 24 for more details on beards and moustaches.

The 1920s

Bright Young Things

1920s WOMEN

The Roaring Twenties were a time of great contrasts. For the Bright Young Things of the monied classes life was one big party swirling with cocktails, jazz and dancing to dawn. But for the less fortunate in Europe and America it was a time of dole queues, hunger marches and depression. By the end of the decade Wall Street had crashed and the UK had experienced a General Strike – the party was over.

As the 1920s progressed most women bobbed and finger waved their hair but the invention of the Marcel wave, the first permanent wave, was a great boon for those with straight hair. In the early 1920s Kurlash eyelash curlers appeared and Pinaud produced mascara "612." In Hollywood, where stars like Theda Bara were becoming major influences for women worldwide, Max Factor received an Academy Award for his Pancromatic foundation, the first award for a make-up product. All fashionable women wore make-up, boldly wearing powder over vanishing creams, strong rouge and kohl round their eyes. The brightly colored lip rouge was applied with two fingers for the top lips and one for the bottom in imitation of Clara Bow "the girl with the bee sting lips." Pale skin still held sway but in Paris the American Josephine Baker's sensational appearance in *Le Revue Negre* generated a fashion for all things African – and tanned skin. By 1925 American women were spending a billion dollars a year on cosmetics and skin care, and fears were being expressed over the safety of cosmetics.

Eye detail

are playing a vamp then highlight your eyelids and use a smudgy charcoal powder close to the lashes.

5 Kohl was extensively used for eyelining. You can use it too but a black or charcoal powder shadow will give the same effect. Remember, if you are working in a large theatre, to leave a gap between the top and bottom eyelines at the corners.

6 Heavy eyelids were fashionable. To create this apply a socket shadow in soft brown.

Keynotes

- early 1920s - pale, heavily powdered skin
- later - more variation in powder colors
- softly arched eyebrows accentuated with pencil
- bright rouge
- kohl rimmed eyes
- small dark red rosebud mouths
- short waved hair

Routine

1 To achieve the fashionable rounded face, use a pale foundation, preferably a more pigmented one like a cake make-up or cream stick.

2 Shade only if your face is naturally plump and needs slimming.

3 Highlight to lose tired shadows.

4 Powder heavily, white was the most popular shade then. Eyeshadow, available in blue, green and turquoise, was used by fast women, but I think blue is the best color for this period on white skins. However, if you

Side view

7 Mascara with black. Cake mascara is more authentic for the period than roll-on.

8 Brush through your eyebrows and round the shape a little with pencil.

9 Rouge was available in many colors but pinks and soft reds are the most useful ones for our needs. Place a circle of bright rouge on each cheek.

10 Lip color came as salves, liquids or in the new metal holders. Three colors were widely available – orange, red and deep rose. Cover your own lips with foundation and draw a small, rounded bow shape.

Optional

False eyelashes were available and considered "essential for vamping," so glamorous characters should have them. Use long, feathery ones rather than heavy thick lashes.

Routine: Black, Darker Skins

Follow the routine but use your normal foundation color. Powder with a toning loose powder. Use a deep red or rose colored rouge. Use a charcoal or smudgy black eyeshadow. Color your mouth with a deep red lipstick, but if your lips are fairly full it would be better to round your own lip shape than attempt a little mouth.

Eye detail: Black, Darker Skins

Routine: Hispanic, Asian

Follow the routine but check to see if a pale foundation suits you, it could either look slightly grey on Hispanic coloring or in the case of broader Asian faces, widen your face.

1920s Men

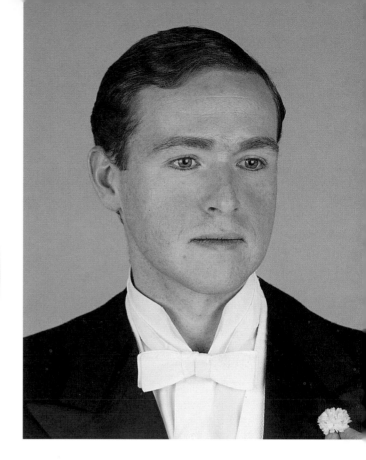

"He was extremely slender and willowy. It was the vogue then for young men of artistic pursuits to appear to be falling apart. And this resemblance to a swaying reed or willow tree gave an impression of fragility, although actually many of them proved unusually durable."

Mercedes de Acosta on Cecil Beaton, 1928

Fashionable young men of the 1920s had money and the time to enjoy it. Others were less fortunate and the rich young undergraduates who manned the trams and trains of the General Strike in the United Kingdom had little comprehension of the miseries of life for much of the working class. The gilded youth of the Jazz Age, men like Cecil Beaton, Evelyn Waugh and Scott Fitzgerald drove Hispano-Suiza's from one party to another and roared down to the South of France to indulge the new craze for sunbathing. Elegant men of this period wore their hair short, usually parted at the side and slicked down. Sideburns were not fashionable and beards and moustaches were generally seen only on older men. "Silly asses" had center partings and wore monocles.

Keynotes

• short, side parted hair, flat to the head

Routine

This is a basic make-up for men. Just add the right hairstyle.

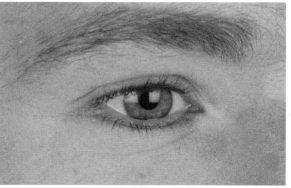

Close-up

The 1930s Woman

Hollywood Style

"From dolls, women of fashion have become works of art"
American *Vogue*, 1933

With the shock of the Depression women rejected the excesses of the 1920s and with it the painted faces. As they returned to the home, leaving jobs free for men, they were told that their responsibility was to be attractive – and good! The ideal image, perfectly represented by Greta Garbo, was one of self-confident but classy sexuality – the goddess. Movie stars became important icons as did society ladies like Wallis Simpson, later Duchess of Windsor, with her cool elegance.

In Hollywood Max Factor created a new foundation, Pancake, for Technicolor® film. Actresses loved it and before long it was available in the high street. In 1932 Revlon created nail varnish and Cutex quickly developed a line of matching lip colors and nail varnishes. With the growing fashion for sunbathing, Ambre Solaire arrived. Throughout the decade lip and cheek colors continued to expand and eyeshadow was available in blue, violet, black and brown. Silver and gold were also fashionable and were often mixed into other colors. Lip brushes were invented and used to draw the cool rounded lips of the period. Fears about the safety of make-up were reinforced when Hollywood star Merle Oberon was badly scarred by make-up poisoning. Hair remained parted at the side and waved, but gradually lengthened until by 1939 chignons and snoods were fashionable.

Keynotes

- high, arched thin eyebrows
- perfectly proportioned bone structure
- coolly bowed dark lips
- smoothly waved or softly curled hair

Routine

1 If you have thick eyebrows they will need blocking out before applying make-up (see page 32).

2 Pale skins, at last, were becoming less fashionable. Tanned skin emphasized white teeth and so darker powders became popular. Pancake make-up came in darker shades and was widely used. You can use it too, choose a straight make-up tone or one slightly darker if appropriate for your character.

3 Perfectly proportioned bone structure was a must for the fashionable woman. Shade your face to accentuate your cheekbones and improve your nose shape.

4 Highlight your cheekbones, the center of your nose and to lose any tired shadows.

5 Powder with a neutral matte, loose powder.

6 They used mainly cream eyeshadows. These are available in theatrical ranges, but you can use powder shadow. Blues and lilacs work well on white skins, blend the color from the lashes right up to the eyebrows. For Hollywood style use silver keeping it to the eyelid area only. Gold is in keeping with the period but looks "flat" under stage lighting.

7 Heavy kohled eyes were definitely unfashionable but subtle eye lining was used. Apply a dark brown line along the edge of the top eyelid and along the roots of the lower lashes. Don't join them up.

8 Mascara with dark brown or black. Brush through to separate your lashes and apply a pair of subtle false lashes.

9 Thin, drawn on arched eyebrows are an absolute must. All fashionable women plucked or shaved their eyebrows. Use black or brown according to your character.

10 Early in the 1930s rouge was out of fashion but gradually it returned. The shape is high on the cheekbones but softer than in the 1920s. Soft red or a deep pink is period.

Close-up

Eye detail

Lips

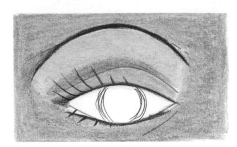

Eye detail: Black, Darker Skins

11 Highly styled lips are important. The shape is still rounded but wider than in the 1920s. Reds in various hues were still the most fashionable lipstick color.

12 Nails were often paler than lips. Darker colors were sometimes used with platinum painted nail tips.

Routine: Black, Darker Skins

Use your normal stage base. Follow the advice for shading and highlighting and powder well. Lilac eyeshadow will work well for this make-up and look in period. Otherwise follow the routine but use black for brows and eyelines. Your lip color should tone with the rouge.

Routine: Hispanic, Asian

Follow the routine but using black pencil, eyeliner and mascara.

The 1930s Man

"Any power whatsoever is destined to fail before fashion."
Benito Mussolini, 1933

The 1930s were a time of sophistication, swing bands, cocktail parties and in Europe, growing political unrest. Unemployment figures in the UK topped three million and thousands of hunger strikers marched on London but now they were joined by well heeled university students. Politics invaded fashionable circles, even *Vogue* magazine devoted space to them; while in Germany and Italy Fascism grew.

Fashionable movie stars, like Fred Astaire and Cary Grant with their elegant style, were admired and copied but the most important influence was the glamorous Prince of Wales. Highly popular with the ordinary people as well as the rich, everything he wore made fashion. Men tied their ties with a "Prince of Wales" knot and wore "Prince of Wales" checks. His abdication to marry an American divorcee in 1937 caused shock waves through the nation.

During this period short hair with a side parting was commonplace. The hair was brushed softly back from the face and held in place with brilliantine. Men were either clean shaven or grew the small neat moustaches made popular by film stars Ronald Coleman and William Powell.

Keynotes

- short hair
- small, narrow moustaches with a gap in the center

Routine

This is a basic straight make-up for all skin colors with an added moustache if appropriate for your character.

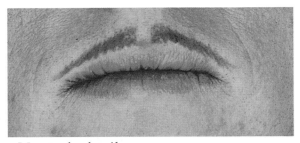

Moustache detail

Make-up lit by footlights

1930s to 1940s

Theatrical Make-up

THEATRICAL MAKE-UP – WOMEN

By the 1930s lighting had become more sophisticated although footlights were still widely used. The dramatic make-ups of Edwardian theatre had developed into a more subtle form. Nevertheless it still looks unusual to us with its little red dots, bright eyeshadows and lipsticks for men. Greasepaint was still the most popular stage make-up but there was growing competition from products originally developed for the Film industry. In 1926 Max Factor, Sr., won an Academy Award for his soft grease make-up which had been created for black and white film, and in 1936 the company launched Pancake especially for Technicolor® film. Still later, in 1938, Panstik was developed for Eastman color film. Actors working in Hollywood liked the new non-greasy foundations and Max Factor launched two ranges especially for the theatre – the N and 20 ranges. Now actors could choose between grease, water-based and cream foundations according to their skin types. I always find it interesting when I look at theatrical photographs to observe how actresses, whilst following basic make-up techniques, always seem to bring the fashionable lipshape and eyebrows with them on stage. You can almost date photographs of productions by that alone. The actresses of these decades did just that. In our photograph the brows and lips are pure 1930s.

Routine

1 You could use greasepaint for this make-up but I would suggest that a pigmented base like Paintstick will give you the same effect. If you choose it, however, you need either No.2 or No.3. The Paintstick color would be 3W. Apply the foundation to give a smooth even effect.

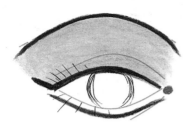

Eye detail

2 Some actresses would have shaded their faces and some didn't – the choice is yours.

3 Apply a medium tone blue cream eyeshadow over your eyelids and right up to your eyebrows.

4 Take a line of white cream shadow along under your lower eyelashes.

5 Powder using a blending powder like Leichner Rose or a good translucent loose powder. Remember to set the eyeshadow as well.

6 With a black or brownish black pencil, depending on your natural hair color or wig, draw thin arched eyebrows. If your own brows are naturally thick you may need to block them out before starting the make-up (see page 32 for the technique).

7 Draw eyelines close to your upper lashes extending them out and up at the outer corners. Take a lower line under the white line beneath your eyes.

8 Mascara with black roll-on or cake. If your character cries during the show choose the cake type, as roll-on mascara would not run if an actress cried properly.

9 Eyelashes can be added at this point for glamour girls. They should be spikey as opposed to thick.

10 Place a dot of red lipstick or lining color next to the inner corners of your eyes – it should be noticeable at distance.

11 Apply a concentrated amount of soft red matte dry rouge to your cheekbones.

12 Color your mouth with red lipstick in a rosebud shape.

13 Blend pancake make-up to match your foundation over your neck and down to the edge of your neck line.

Routine: Black, Darker Skins

Use a foundation to match your own skin and powder with a tinted, as opposed to a translucent, loose powder which will give a more matte finish and look more theatrical. I suggest either lilac or green eyeshadow, rather than blue, and a really scarlet lipstick.

Close-up

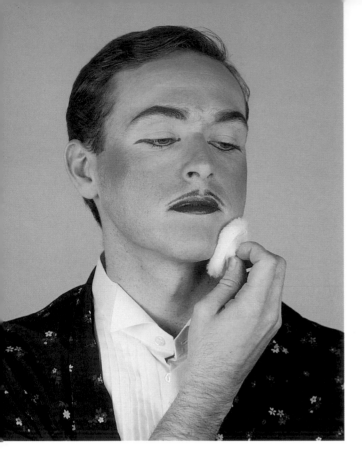

Eye detail

THEATRICAL MAKE-UP – MEN

This is the period of the elegant and sophisticated stage productions of Noël Coward and Ivor Novello. It is also a time when male actors wore what today we might consider somewhat feminine make-up. There were set make-ups for most characters and a difference in the make-up for older leading men and the juvenile lead. This, however, is the basic male routine.

Routine

1 You can use greasepaint, cream stick or cake make-up, the important thing is to make the face look noticeably covered in foundation. Choose a brighter or more tanned color than you would normally.

2 Men used blue eyeshadow in the same way as women. A cream shadow is the best option because you want a matte finish and powder ones often contain shimmer. Blend it from the roots of your eyelashes right up to your eyebrows; the blue should be a medium tone. If you use cream apply it before powdering, with powder shadows powder your eyelids first.

3 Powder lavishly with neutral or translucent loose powder. If you are using a cream stick or greasepaint for the first time they need to be very well set or they can quickly become shiny.

4 Draw a black line under your eyes and using either black or dark brown pencil define your eyebrows clearly. At this time character was often indicated by strong eyebrows.

5 Brush some bright red rouge on to the center of your cheeks. You could also use a little red greasepaint but this is best done before you powder.

Close-up

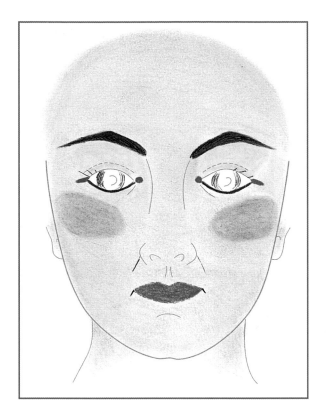

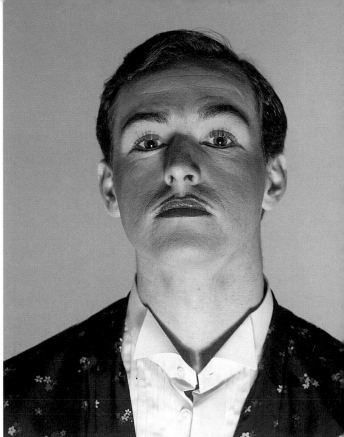

Make-up lit by footlights

6 It was standard practice for men and women to have red dots at the inner corners of their eyes. This was usually done with Carmine greasepaint but some men used lipstick or cream liner instead. The dots should be quite noticeable, their function was to brighten the eyes.

7 With the same cosmetic draw a short line from the outer corner of each eye.

8 Men wore red lipstick on stage. It can stain your lips as it is very pigmented so you may prefer to use a red lining color or greasepaint stick which will not.

Routine: Black, Darker Skins

A compressed powder to match your skin applied heavily will give a matte theatrical look. Rather than blue shadow use lilac. Eyebrows and eyelines are black and you will need a deep red lip color and rouge.

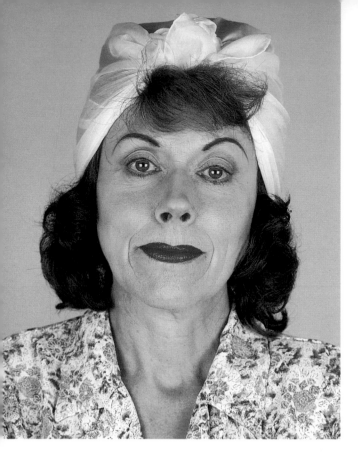

The 1940s

War in Europe

"We must never forget that good looks and good morale are the closest of good companions. Put your best face forward!"
Wartime Yardley Advertising

WARTIME WOMEN

With the declaration of war, make-up production ceased in the UK and the factories were turned over to the war effort. In the USA production was restricted until in 1943 an official report recommended that the establishment of well-stocked powder rooms in factories could boost production by 10 to 15 percent. Nevertheless cosmetics did become scarce with lipstick cited as the item most missed. Soon the British Government also realized the morale boosting potential of cosmetics but supplies were still severely restricted. As always, women used their imaginations and applied Vaseline to their eyelids and, as silk stockings quickly disappeared, colored their legs with tanned make-up and penciled a line up the backs to simulate seams. When war finally ended in 1945, despite rationing, Christian Dior's extravagant New Look, with yards of skirt and tight fitted jackets, gradually swept away the wide shouldered, short skirted economy fashions of wartime.

Close-up of lips

Keynotes

- matte, powdered skin
- thin, penciled eyebrows with the arches positioned towards the temples
- wide, bowed lips in strong reds
- elaborate rolled hairstyles worn up or shoulder length

Routine

1 Thick eyebrows will require blocking out, sometimes only the outer ends will need hiding (see page 32).

2 The skin should look smooth and velvety for fashionable women, so cake make-up and cream sticks give the best effect. However, you could use a less covering base for unfashionable characters. The skin should generally appear healthy.

3 Shade and highlight to improve your facial structure but, unless your eyelids are narrow or set back, leave out the shading on your browbone.

4 Powder well – remember this was a key element in the 1940s and the face should reflect this.

5 In the USA colored eyeshadow was available but in Europe Vaseline was popular, cheap and effective – it created a shine on the lids which made the eyes appear larger. You can try it but a cream powder highlighter will give the same effect without the greasiness. Blend it over the whole eyelid.

Eye detail

6 For larger stages apply top and bottom eyelines but for smaller theatres just run a faded line along the roots of the lower lashes.

7 Cake mascara applied with a wet brush was used to color the eyelashes. Still available it darkens them while keeping them well separated.

8 Eyebrows should look definitely penciled, powder brow make-up is useless for this. Draw an arched shape with the high point of the arch towards the sides of the face.

9 Cream rouge was widely used but for economy some women used a little lipstick instead. Apply three dots and blend into a triangular shape before powdering your face. You can, of course, also use matte blusher to do this. Soft red, coral or pink are good color choices.

10 Outline the lips in a wide bow shape and fill in with strong red or one with a bluey tone. For a really hard look, copy Joan Crawford's tough lip shape.

Optional

- for more glamour add a pair of spikey false lashes
- beauty spots were popular – draw one on your cheek with black pencil

Routine: Black, Darker Skins

Follow the routine adjusting foundations, eyebrow, eyeline, lipstick and rouge to suit your skin tone.

The 1940s Woman

Hollywood Glamour

"We used to admire the artificial woman and the sophisticated woman of fashion. What we want now is the outdoor girl."
Max Factor, Sr., 1938

During the difficult years of the 1940s with restrictions in place on both sides of the Atlantic, Hollywood continued to be a major influence on make-up and hairstyles as well as an important morale booster. It is impossible to write about this period without mentioning Max Factor. The Factor family arrived in America, from Russia, in 1909 and by 1920 Max Factor, Sr., was established in Hollywood designing the make-up for stars like Theda Bara, Pola Negri and Clara Bow, the "It" girl, as well as training men like the Westmore brothers whose work was to be dominant in movies for decades to come. Factor and his sons continued to create the images for actresses like Jean Harlow, Rita Hayworth and Joan Crawford whom he teased about the thickness of the foundation she used to hide her freckles. By the end of the 1930s color film had arrived. It gave women the chance to see what the stars were using and they wanted it too. The company shrewdly marketed a day range Society Make-up, carefully named for the ladylike image, and advertised it with movie stars like Bette Davis, Ginger Rogers and Myrna Loy. The grateful stars asked no payment. Soon ordinary women were using Panstik and Pancake too. In pursuit of a more "natural" look the fashionable face looked healthier but still smooth, eyebrows thickened but still arched and rouge became triangular in position. Lips, however, were anything but natural – scarlet, wide bows and epitomized at their most extreme by Joan Crawford's powerful mouth. Hair was grown longer and was dressed in elaborate rolls, put up or waved down covering one eye like Veronica Lake's.

Keynotes

- healthy but powdered skin
- arched, penciled eyebrows
- overdrawn, bowed lips
- flowers and bows worn in elaborate hairstyles

Routine

1 As with the previous look a fashionable woman's foundation would give a noticeably made up appearance. The most popular foundations of the day, the stick and cake make-ups, give this look perfectly. Choose the stick for normal and dry skins and cake for combination or greasy skins. Apply like warpaint and blend to give an even finish, add more as necessary. The skin tone should look healthy. Some over made-up women looked quite orangey, this could be interesting for some characters.

2 Shade and highlight but if your eyes are naturally large leave out the shading above your eyelids.

3 Apply a mid toned blue cream eyeshadow or liner over your eyelids. Powder eyeshadows have too much shimmer in them for this time.

4 Powder well, preferably with a matte loose powder. In the 1940s powders matched foundation colours which gave a different look. A blending powder like Leichner's Rose would work well. Pancake can be powdered with Creme Puff or any compact powder.

5 Draw a fine line along your top eyelids, using dark brown or black as appropriate, extending it out a little at the corners for larger theatres. Draw another line under your eyes. Add a soft socket shadow to define your eyelids. Mascara carefully separating the eyelashes and apply a pair of fine spikey false eyelashes.

6 Eyebrows were no longer heavily plucked but still arched with the high point now further to the sides of the brows. They were noticeably penciled.

7 Rouge was important and was worn in a triangular shape close to the nose. Women used cream rouge in three dots blending them together (do this before powdering) or brush on matte powder rouge. The color toned with the lipstick.

Eye detail

Close-up

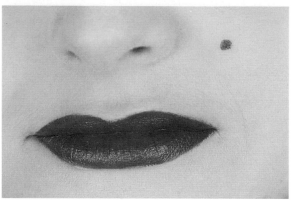

Lips

Eye detail: Black, Darker Skins

8 The lip shape is a focal point of this make-up. In 1946 American women spent 30 million dollars on lipstick and during restrictions it was the most longed for cosmetic. Deep reds, scarlets and pinky reds were popular and the shape is slightly overdrawn and bowed at the sides of the top lip. Glycerine was used to give gloss to the mouth.

Routine: Black, Darker Skins

Use your own foundation with a matching tinted powder. Green eyeshadow and a deep scarlet mouth completes the look.

The 1940s Man

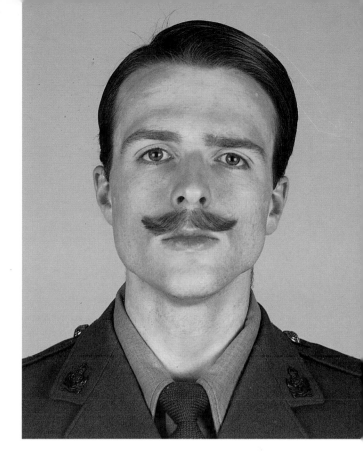

"Use it up, wear it out, make it do or do without."
USA Government Slogan

War in Europe brought clothes rationing to Britain in 1941 and shoe rationing in America by 1943. With increasing numbers of men joining or being conscripted into the forces hairstyles in Europe and the USA became pretty standardized. The British Army had its regulation "short back and sides" and only the glamorous young RAF pilots got away with longer hair – though it wouldn't seem long to our eyes. They became known as the "Brylcreem Boys" from their use of a popular hair cream of the time. Most men wore their hair parted at the side and brushed back, two brushes were used – one in each hand. Most men were clean shaven although there were notable exceptions like Adolf Hitler and General de Gaulle. Some RAF types sported handlebar moustaches, some senior Army officers had neat slightly upturned ones and British "spivs" (black marketeers) were known to wear narrow shapes. Very few young men wore beards even after the end of World War II but some men, too old for the forces, grew them. After peace was declared there was no noticable change in men's hairstyles.

Keynotes

- short hair, side parted and greased down
- regulation military haircuts

Routine

This is a basic straight make-up for all ethnic groups.

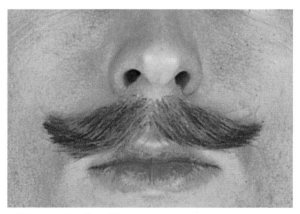

Moustache detail

The 1950s Woman

Sophistication

"Most women lead lives of dullness, of quiet desperation. Cosmetics are a wonderful escape from it - if you play it right."
Martin Revson, Vice-president of Revlon, 1952

Although there was austerity and rationing in the UK until well into the 1950s, the New Look created in 1947 had already influenced make-up and hairstyles. In 1953 Max Factor produced Creme Puff - the first all in one make-up – it was a huge success, a year later they introduced the concealer Erace. In this period aerosols were invented and Rubenstein's mascara wand Mascaramatic appeared.

The face of this period was still quite made-up with unlifted "doe" eyes and more angled eyebrows and lips. Hair was dressed up in French pleats, cut very short or set in more elaborate styles like the Italian Boy style popularized by Gina Lollobrigida.

The ideal woman, epitomized by Grace Kelly, was perfectly groomed, beautifully dressed, immaculately made-up and elegantly coiffured. But a revolution was brewing – the advent of the teenager.

Eye detail

Keynotes

- doc eyes – top eyelines sharply extended
- angled penciled eyebrows
- coolly pointed lips
- nail varnish to match lipstick

Routine

1 Use a straight stage base. The face should look naturally healthy unless the character is highly fashionable in which case she should look a little paler and well powdered.

2 Shade and highlight to improve your facial structure.

3 I think the eyeshadow colors that epitomize the 1950s are greens and greys, although older women still clung to blues. The shadow goes over the lids and then sweeps out and up at the sides. You can use powder or creme shadow.

4 Set with loose powder before the powder eyeshadow but after using cream shadow. Powders that matched foundation colors were still widely used giving a more matte

look to the face. Creme Puff was used as an all-in-one make-up (and still is), if you want to try it choose a color to match your skin tone but a little darker if you are very pale.

5 The doe eye is key to the fashionable face of this decade. The top lid is lined with black or dark brown pencil with the extension flicking up sharply at the outer corners, it was said to emulate a deer's eye shape. In social make-up there was usually no emphasis of the bottom lid but for medium to large theatres I recommend a softly faded underline.

6 Cake mascara was still widely used but with the advent of mascara wands (roll-on mascaras) women could achieve thicker lashes quickly. Most women only mascared their top lashes. Models and glamour girls wore false lashes, apply them after you mascara. Marilyn Monroe wore half lashes from the center lid outwards which works well with "doe" eyes.

7 Pencil in your eyebrows following the shape in the diagram.

Close-up

Lips

Eye detail: Black, Darker Skins

8 Rouge colors were becoming much more muted now and corals and peaches more fashionable than reds. Teenage girls concentrated more on eyes and lips leaving out the rouge. The right position is along the high point of the cheekbones. Although powder rouges came with little pads to apply them, models were starting to use brushes instead.

9 Lipstick was still the number 1 cosmetic for all women but colors were changing. The brilliant "Fire and Ice" red that was a huge American seller for Revlon was giving way to softer pinks and corals.

10 Paint your nails to match your lipstick.

Routine: Black, Darker Skins

Use your usual stage base and follow the routine replacing brown with black in eyeliner, brow make-up and mascara. Few cosmetics were formulated for darker skins even then, so Black and darker skinned women often resorted to theatrical ranges to find the right colors. Use deeper clear reds for lips and cheeks and green eyeshadow.

The 1950s Woman

The Sex Kitten

The high fashion 1950s saw a new, and important, phenomenon – the advent of the teenager. For the first time young people had a little money to spend and they used it to identify themselves as a group in society. Despite disapproving parents, sixteen year-olds began to use lipstick and eye make-up in Europe, something already established in America. Teenage girls wore Sloppy Joes and tight jeans or jumpers tucked into full skirts floating over layers of net petticoats. They jived in jazz clubs, listened to skiffle or the new rock and roll. Their idols were the elfin Audrey Hepburn with her boyish figure and short gamin hair cut and the sensational young Brigitte Bardot with her childish pout and provacative figure, half woman, half child – the sex kitten.

Keynotes

- healthy lightly tanned skins
- uptilted eyelines and eyebrows
- pale lips and nails
- gamin hair cuts or pony tails

Routine

1 In contrast to the matte Sophistication make-up this face should glow with health. Unless it is unsuitable for your character choose a slightly tanned base.

2 Shade to improve your bone structure being sure to apply it to the brow bones.

3 Highlight to remove tired shadows and improve bone structure.

4 Highlight your eyelids.

5 Powder the whole face well with translucent loose powder.

6 Line your eyelids with black pencil or cake eyeliner extending the lines out and upwards sharply at the outer corners into elongated triangles. Sophia Loren always started her extensions slightly before the corners which gave a strong tilt to her eyes.

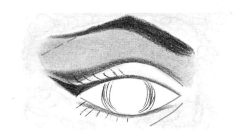

Eye detail

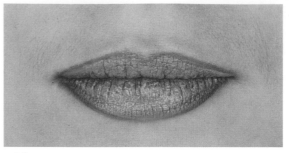

Lips

9 Using a peachy tone rouge blend a little color close to your hairline on your cheekbones and fade it along a little and into your cheek shading. This is optional.

10 Bardot popularized very pale chalky lip colors with a pinky tone, the shape is full and pouty. Lip liners and pencils had not been invented so fashionable girls outlined their lips with brown eyebrow pencil.

Eye detail: Black, Darker Skins

7 Girls who did line their bottom lids used the same color, joining the lines up at the outer corners, but this is only advisable for small venues as it can make your eyes appear smaller on stage. Mascara your top lashes *only* with black. Apply a brown socket shadow lifting it to follow the eyeline angle at the outer corners.

8 Brush through your eyebrows and color them making a more angular uplifted shape.

Routine: Black, Darker Skins

Follow the routine using colors suitable for your own coloring but don't try a very pale lipstick, instead use a slightly lighter color than usual lining it with a deep lipliner.

Close-up

The 1950s Man

The James Dean Influence

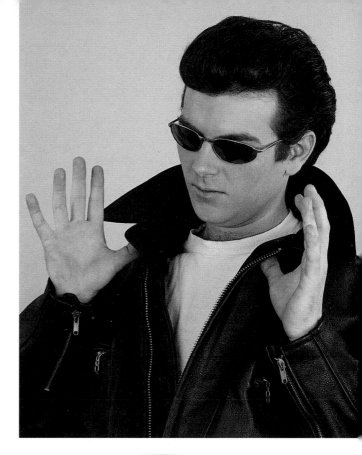

After the greyness of post war England the most noticeable fashion change came about among young working class men and was street generated. They adapted the elegant Edwardian styles of Savile Row into a more exaggerated look with velvet collared, long drape jackets, drainpipe trousers and heavy crepe soled "brothel creepers." In contrast to the short hairstyles favored by most men in 1953, hair was long at the back, thickly greased with exaggerated quiffs and worn with long sideburns. Greased hair and more moderate quiffs with sideburns were also sported by young men copying James Dean, Elvis Presley and other Hollywood stars whose images popularized the casual image of jeans, T-shirts and leather jackets. Clean cut young Americans wore short hair, still parted but no longer greased down, and Ivy League suits. Curly brimmed bowler hats were worn with elegant Savile Row suits in London. Fashion conscious men everywhere were generally clean shaven.

Keynotes

- short hair with side parting but either worn naturally or held in shape with light brilliantines. Brylcreem was still used but not by fashionable men
- short sideburns with hair styled with a quiff at front
- moustaches were out of fashion, as were beards

> *"You can express yourself like, in clothes; you know a nice dark red shirt with black verticals and a dark blue suit, a Perry Como and Italians, you're in there, sharp, playing it cool."*
> 17-year-old, *Vogue*, 1959

Teddy Boys

- hair grown down the neck and very long at the front and swept over the forehead and back in an exaggerated quiff. Long sideburns. No beard or moustache.

Routine

This is a basic stage make-up with a quiffed hairstyle and sideburns. See page 25 for more detail on supplementing sideburns.

The 1960s

Swinging London

1960s Women

In the 1960s in America a vibrant young President John F. Kennedy with his glamorous wife and perfect family became a symbol of youthful hope. London took over from Paris as the center of Fashion and for the first time youth took control of style. Talented and creative designers, photographers, models, hairdressers, make-up artists, actors and pop stars in their twenties dictated what people wore and how they looked. They came from all kinds of backgrounds and broke all the rules, London's youth culture exploded influencing the world.

Young (and not so young) women joyfully flung themselves into Mary Quant's revolutionary mini skirts and her first USA tour stopped the traffic on Broadway with its long legged models.

Make-up became highly stylized, influenced by photographs of top models like Jean Shrimpton and later Twiggy. Looking back it seems astoundingly heavy with its eyelines and loads of lashes but at the time all fashionable women wore a version of it. American Flori Roberts created the first make-up range for Black women and Rubenstein invented waterproof mascara. At the beginning of the decade hair rose in height and was dressed into "beehive" styles or crowned with a bunch of false curls often decorated with ribbons or flowers. However, Vidal Sassoon's beautifully cut short geometric styles with their heavy fringes were also very influential. During this time wigs, hairpieces and false eyelashes, often made from real hair, were a *must*.

Keynotes

- heavy, heavy top and bottom eyelines plus a noticeable socket shadow. Later, influenced by Twiggy, eyelashes were drawn under the eyes.
- false eyelashes - it is impossible to recreate this period without them. The height of fashion was two pairs on the top lid and one pair underneath.

Eye detail

Eye detail: Black, Darker Skins

- "rouge" disappeared and was reborn as "blusher." A browny tone was worn under the cheekbones and it was noticeable.
- beehive hairstyles – French pleats with an added piece on top, short Vidal Sassoon asymmetrical cuts – back combing

Routine

1 Apply foundation using your normal stage base – the skin should look healthy. Sunbathing became fashionable so a tanned look would be appropriate for some characters.

2 Shade and highlight as in your straight make-up but use highlight on your lids and right up to your eyebrows.

3 Powder. Translucent loose powder, which was used in the film industry and popularized by models, was launched into everyday make-up ranges in the 1960s. Powder particularly well along the eyelash roots otherwise you may have difficulty gluing your false lashes on later.

4 Apply powder blusher in a warm brown tone along the edge of your cheekbones and into the hollows beneath them. Suck in your cheeks to find the position. The blusher should look strong.

5 The trendiest eyeshadow was white, sometimes available in stick form, but aqua, green and blue were also popular. If you choose a color like green apply that to your eyelids and white on the brow bone above your lids. For our needs powder shadow is fine but should you choose to use white, a cream type would be better as white powder defuses the strength of the eyeliner.

6 Very fashionable women wore black eyeliner and the more elegant used brownish black. London models wore Max Factor cake make-up 2880 (still available in the Kryolan range), applied with a Chinese brush, and later in the 60s liquid liner. You can use either, but always draw the top line first taking it out from the eye corners in an elongated triangle. The bottom line comes out at the corner too but is shorter. Using a charcoal powder shadow or cake liner, add a strong socket shadow, and don't soften it.

7 Roll-on mascara appeared around this time and it was fashionable to mascara top and bottom eyelashes heavily - black for serious trendies, brownish black for everyone else.

8 Apply false lashes to top lid. They should be thick not feathery. If you have difficulties, cut them in half - its easier to fix them on that way. Mascara them carefully into your own lashes.

9 Eyebrows were underplayed so just feather them in lightly with powder eyebrow make-up.

10 Lip colors varied but generally a pale or peachy tone combined with a darker outline in pencil looks good. The top lip shape is natural but slightly overdrawn at the outer corners. Blot color and add lipgloss.

Optional

A second pair of top lashes. Underlashes or (later in period) drawn on lashes under the eyes. Underlashes are glued *underneath* your own lower lashes not on top of them.

Close-up

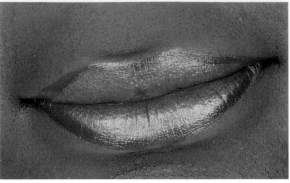

The mouth

Routine: Black, Darker Skins

White eyeshadow looks very strong on a darker skin tone like our model's so I used a pale aqua which looks better and is still in period. Browny blusher may not show up so either use a deep rusty tone or leave it out. Be careful with lipgloss unless you want to look like the Supremes, and obviously pale lip colors are not for you.

THE TWIGGY IMPACT

Before Twiggy, English models traditionally were middle-class, not noticeably thin and looked older than their age. Indeed so did most young girls then. But the chirpy, streetwise cockney teenager broke this model forever. Her skinny vulnerable look perfectly symbolized Swinging London's youthful image and she became an instant success and an icon for young women.

   Twiggy was photographed during her career with many hairstyles. The one in the photograph is the very popular combination of a French pleat (see page 30) combined with a false top knot worn widely in the 1960s.

Close-up

Eye detail

Routine

This is the make-up that she made world famous. It differs from the previous one mainly in the eyeshadow color, the paler lips and, most importantly, the lashes drawn under the eyes.

Routine Black, Darker Skins

Refer to Swinging London make-up section, page 98, but add drawn on underlashes.

Eye detail: Black, Darker Skins

1960s MEN

In the 1960s men began to break away from the dull styles of the 1950s. Even conservative Englishmen became more fashion conscious wearing kipper ties and "Italian Style" suits with their shorter jackets and tapered pants. The "Hooray Henrys" of the Establishment wore sheepskin jackets, cavalry twills and paisley cravats. The explosion of youth culture was a major influence on young men worldwide. The Beatles' clean-cut image of collarless suits and heavy fringes spawned a million lookalikes, as did the Rolling Stones with their loose satin frilled shirts, skin-tight trousers and unkempt hair.

In the early 1960s hair remained short but side partings were becoming less noticeable as men ceased to grease it down. Gradually hair began to lengthen at the back and short sideburns appeared. Moustaches and beards were still unfashionable and most men were clean-shaven until the advent of Flower Power in America and the arrival of the Hippie look later in the decade. When this happened hair was grown even longer and some young men wore painted facial symbols.

Keynotes

Early 1960s
- hair short but creeping below the ears at the back, worn with short sideburns. Brylcreem was still used but fashionable men either relied on a good cut or used something lighter
- moustaches and beards – most men were clean shaven so keep them for unfashionable characters, e.g., an English colonel would probably sport a moustache

Routine

Make-up – this is a straight stage make-up.

POP INFLUENCES

The Beatles
- pudding basin haircut or wig with heavy fringe, short at back with short sideburns

Rolling Stones
- hair below ears, fringed but untidy. (Later the fringe goes and the hair lengthens.)

The 1970s Woman

High Fashion

"What better time to paint your face, paint your hair, your boots, your body?"
Vogue, 1970

The protest movement in America in the late 1960s, with its "make love not war" slogan was, in the decade that followed, to have a profound influence on fashion. Espoused by pop stars like Janis Joplin and John Lennon its street style was to influence the world of couture. No longer did young people follow fashion – they created it. Flower Power, from America, with its painted faces and bodies, and brightly colored caftans and beads, translated into the wonderfully patterned clothes of designers like Zandra Rhodes; Ethnic became High Fashion. The fashion store Biba in London, with its nostalgic 1930s frocks sent girls everywhere scouring second-hand shops and their Grandmothers' wardrobes for period outfits. The anarchic look of punks with their unhealthy pale faces, black rimmed eyes, Mohican hair styles and brutal clothes, still influence young designers today. With the interest in other cultures, top models like Beverley Johnson, the first black woman to appear on the cover of *Vogue*, were in demand.

Facially the 1970s saw an explosion of color. Make-up articles showed faces painted like rainbows. In practical terms this meant fashionable women using several different eyeshadow colors on their eyelids; for example shimmering blues, lilacs and pinks and blended around and under the eyes. Colored mascaras were popular too. The move later in the decade towards a concern for the environment led to a layered country style fashion and less colorful make-up. Permed Afro hairstyles were very popular with both men and women and many young men grew their hair long.

Keynotes
- natural or tanned skin
- shimmering eyeshadows used in groups of colors, pink was popular combined with lilac and blue
- thin eyebrows
- browny blusher under cheekbones with a different tone on bones
- hair long, medium length, natural shapes – later mid-length and flicked back like Farah Fawcett Major's, or cut very short like Liza Minelli's in the film *Cabaret*

Close-up, eye make-up

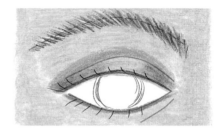

Eye detail

Routine

1 Use either a standard base, or since sun-bathing was very popular, a tan tone.

2 Improve your face shape as necessary with shader and highlight.

3 Powder with translucent loose powder making sure that you set the foundation on your eyelids well.

4 This is the era when shimmer eyeshadows appeared. The trendy English companies like Mary Quant and Biba produced brilliant palettes of color and Madeleine Mono made little pots of iridescent powder shadow. The most popular color combination mixed pink, blue and lilac. Blend a pale pink powder shadow over the whole lid area and up to your eyebrows.

5 With an applicator or brush apply a deeper lilac to both sides of the eyelids leaving the center pink. Smudge the lilac around the outer corners and run a blue line along under your eyes – it should look misty.

6 With a deeper blue, accentuate the edge of the socket bone fading it slightly upwards. Fade the dark blue into the lilac at the outer

eye corners. I know it seems complicated but it is easier to do than you think!

7 Mascara with dark brown, black or, for small stages, navy blue. Eyelashes were sometimes added but the thick false ones of the 1960s were out of fashion and were replaced by softer, natural styles.

8 Eyebrows were quite thin and little attention was paid to them, just brush them through.

9 Cheeks were still contoured. To achieve this use a browny blusher beneath the cheekbones. Then brush a pinkier blusher along the cheekbones to give natural color.

10 Frosted lipsticks arrived in the 1970s and the colors went from pale to mid tones, dark lips were unfashionable until Biba produced plum tones to go with its ethereal, nostalgic fashions. There is no strong shape in this period but the top lip is more rounded than in the 1960s.

Routine: Black, Darker Skins

Make-up ranges for darker skins were still very limited in England although things were improving in America. To recreate this period

Eye detail: Black, Darker Skinned women

use your normal stage foundation, shader and highlight. You can just follow the eye make-up routine using those colors or replace the blues with dark lilac, blending it into the pinks where the blues are used on the eyelids. Choose a blusher and lip color with strong rose overtones to continue the pink feel of the make-up.

1970s Man

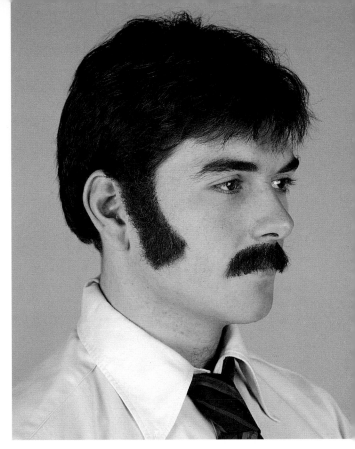

"The real star of the fashion picture now is the wearer."
Vogue, 1974

With ethnic and secondhand clothes dominating female styles in the 1970s, male fashion, perhaps for the first time, divided. Many men, particularly the older generations, remained devoted to their suits albeit now with flared trousers and worn with large pointed collars on their shirts and kipper ties. But, with growing environmental concern and increasing interest in alternative life styles young men took to the relaxed, patched and embroidered fashions of Hippiedom. The single medallion of the swinging 60s became strings of beads and some men pierced one ear and wore an earring, something not seen since the seventeenth century. John Lennon abandoned his Beatles' image and wore a beard, moustache, and long, straight hair parted in the center. Pop idol David Essex, star of *Godspell*, grew his hair long and layered with a soft fringe whilst Marc Bolan of T. Rex was a riot of

dark curls. Both were clean shaven. Some young men chose Afro styles and permed their hair. More conventional men were also influenced and hair generally was worn below the ear and forward with long side whiskers. Thick moustaches modeled on that of Ché Guevara were very popular.

Keynotes

- full, soft hair often with a fringe
- side whiskers grown to below the ears
- full natural moustaches

Routine

This is a basic make-up with an added moustache and side whiskers for most characters.

The 1970s

Hippies

Hippie culture, with its free love and anti-war stance, was an important influence in the early 1970s although it had its roots in the late 1960s with the protests against the Vietnam War in America. Hippies were generally young and they rejected society's attitude to how you should live, what you should think, what you should wear and most importantly what was good for the planet. Like punk, the hippie style was highly individual. It was also inexpensive, recycling second-hand clothes and customizing outfits with patches, appliqué and embroidery. The interest in Ethnic clothes, jewelery and hairstyles began with the Hippies. They grew their hair long or permed it Afro style; girls plaited it and wove in beads, feathers and flowers. Facially women and some men used kohl to emphasize their eyes and painted symbols, flowers and African style stripes on their cheeks. These simple face decorations influenced the make-up world for a time with high fashion women's magazines advocating elaborate and totally impractical make-ups. Like John Lennon, many young men grew naturally shaped beards and moustaches.

Keynotes

- natural or tanned skin
- kohl eye make-up
- facial decorations
- long hair or permed Afro styles
- men – shaggy beards and moustaches

Routine

1 Apply foundation choosing a healthy tanned base. Those with darker skins, like the model, shouldn't need one.

2 Highlight your eyelids to make your eyes appear larger.

3 Whatever your skin tone powder the face, especially your eyelids.

4 Using a kohl pencil or charcoal powder shadow draw faded eyelines close to your top eyelashes and under your lower ones. Be careful not to join them up or your eyes will look smaller.

5 Paint designs on your cheeks using Aquacolor or other face paints. I chose the symbol of the CND movement for one side and stripes for the other. As I used red for the symbol it needed a black outline to make it stand out on stage.

6 Add an Afro wig or a long straight one with a center parting.

Optional

With the long wig – a shaggy beard or moustache.
　　Tie an Ethnic print scarf around your head.

Female Hippie

This Hippie is male but the simple design can be adapted for women. Generally female Hippies wore little make-up concentrating on dark rimmed eyes although some did wear very pale lipstick. So do a straight "no-make-up" make-up using a light tanned foundation. Add a long wig and plait the front or do this to your own hair. Flowers, beads or small feathers can be attached to the plaits.

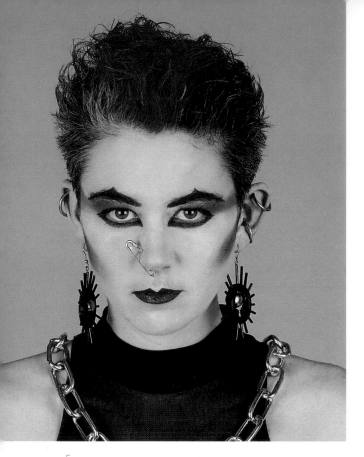

The 1970s

Punks

Punk culture exploded on to London streets in the mid 1970s, sending shock waves through conservative Britain. Its confrontational, anarchic look was in stark contrast to the gentle Ethnic and retro styles fashionable at the time. Punks wore black leather, rubber, bondage collars and chains. With their unhealthy pale faces, voodooish make-up and strange brightly colored or jet black hair styles, they looked both provocative – and threatening.

Female punks and some boys used the pale, pale make-up we have seen in past centuries and girls wore highly stylized black eye make-up and eyebrows with dark lipsticks. Some male punks used eye make-up too. Both sexes bleached their hair and sprayed it with bright primary colors or dyed it jet black. The most popular male haircuts harked back to the Mohican styles of Native America, the more exotic cuts were held in place with sugar syrup. Ears and noses were pierced with often a safety pin through one nostril. Punk style, which is still around

today and a continuing influence on young fashion, is highly individual and no two punks look the same.

Keynotes

- white or very pale foundation
- black eye make-up and eyebrows
- black or dark red lipstick
- tattoos – black or brightly colored

This make-up contains the key elements and could be adapted for male use e.g. cut out the rouge and lipstick, and reduce the eye make-up.

Routine

1 Apply white or a very pale foundation. The face should look stark but not clown-like.

2 Powder well.

Close-up

3 Using a plum or brown toned blusher shade under your cheekbones, the position is described in the 1960s section.

4 Following the chart blend dark grey powder eyeshadow from your socket to your eyebrows and out to your hairline.

5 Outline your eyes with black pencil or a liner, pointing the inner corners slightly downwards. This makes your eyes look smaller but in this stylized make-up it doesn't matter. Mascara heavily with black.

6 Draw sharply angular eyebrows. If you bring them closer together you will look fiercer.

7 Color your mouth with either scarlet, deep browny red, deep plum or black lipstick. The shape should be hard and pointed.

Eye detail

Optional

We cut a safety pin, stretched it and put it on one nostril – you don't have to pierce your nose to look authentic!

Routine: Black, Darker Skins

You rarely see black Punks and indeed the look does depend on the pale skin. However, a combination of heavy black eye make-up, dark lips and a brightly colored hairstyle or wig could give a feel of Punk style to a darker skin.

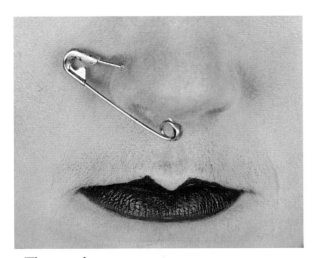

The mouth

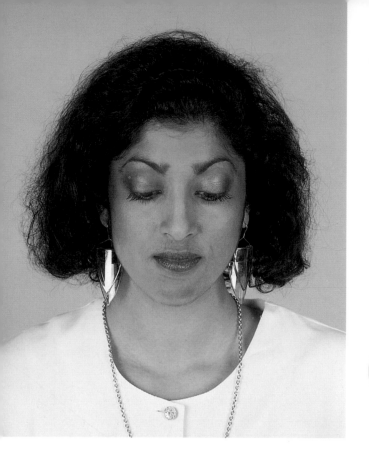

The 1980s

Power Dressing

> *"I like a lot of make-up, I believe in it for beauty and protection."*
> Joan Collins, *Ladies Home Journal*

1980s WOMEN

In the UK, under the leadership of Margaret Thatcher, conspicuous consumerism was the order of the day and symbols of success became important. This was particularly so in the fashion world where suddenly everything had to have a designer label. Young women were becoming increasingly economically independant and many older women returned to the work place. This change was reflected by the fashions of the time. Power dressing with its emphasis on strong little suits and dresses became popular. Shoulder pads, rarely seen since the 1940s, were back in fashion and used for everything. This masculine shoulder line was countered by big, fluffy hair and chunky earrings. The great icon of this look, and a major influence on High Street fashion was Joan Collins as Alexis in the American television series *Dynasty* with her tough but highly glamorous clothes. In the

USA fashion became more classic but it was an American, Norma Kamali, who introduced the other big fashion of the decade – exercise clothes. Since the late 1970s there had been a craze for exercise; dance studios and gyms were big business in Europe and the USA. Kamali took the practical sports outfits and made them couture. Bob Marley, wearing tracksuits on stage, influenced a whole generation of young black men.

In the 1980s Elizabeth Arden had its biggest seller ever with Lip Fix and men began to use moisturizer and hair gel. The dominant color in make-up was brown, brown and more brown introduced by make-up designers like Barbara Daly. Ultra Glow, an all purpose tan powder, became a huge seller. You could use it as foundation, blusher, eyeshadow or lip color. Tinted moisturizers were widely used combined with reddish brown powder shadow, brownish blusher and lipstick in plums or brown tones. Although big hair was fashionable there were many casual "wash and go" styles. Men's hair was generally short and beards and moustaches were unfashionable.

Keynotes

- brown eyeshadow
- shimmery, brown powder as a foundation
- browny blusher taken over the cheekbones and up into the temples
- flat brown lipstick or plum tones

Routine

1 At the beginning of this decade sun-bathing was still popular and a suntan fashionable, so if it is appropriate for your character choose a light tanned foundation. Ultra Glow, was widely used to give skin a healthy glow but this type of sheeny make-up will make your skin look too shiny on stage so if you want that type of effect apply a little, after powdering, on to your cheek-bones and down the center of your nose. This will give that look in a controlled way. If you don't want to look tanned use a straight base in a healthy tone.

2 Shade and highlight to improve your facial structure and powder the whole face with translucent powder.

3 Brown eyeshadow remained popular for white skins for most of the 1980s and well into the 1990s. Reddy browns were favoured and later the more muted grey browns. This is a difficult color for the stage as it makes your eyes appear smaller, so it is very important that you only use a pale brown on your eyelids and keep the deeper tones for the socket shadow and under the eyes (on medium to large stages this will need to be combined with a top and bottom eyeline for definition and a pair of soft eyelashes). Apply the pale brown to the whole lid and then blend a richer brown along the socket bone and on to the eyelid at the outer corner. Blend some along under the eyes fading the color off as you come to the center.

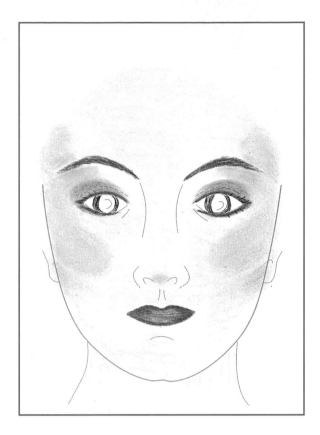

4 Mascara your top and bottom lashes well using brown or black.

5 During this decade powder eyebrow make up appeared giving the brows soft definition. By all means use it but just remember not to rub your eyebrow by mistake. There is no special shape for the 1980s, natural brows were in.

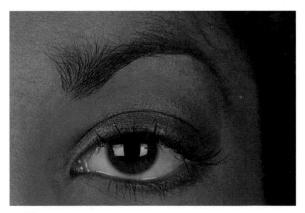

Close-up

Eye detail

Eye detail: Black, Darker Skins

6 Blusher became rusty in tone at this time and was applied with very big, fat brushes. It was taken over the cheekbones and up on to the temples; and sometimes the brow bone as well, as a kind of eyeshadow. If you have a thin face this position will actually make it look thinner so beware!

7 Tinted lipglosses were developed in the 1980s but they are not much use for theatre. The most popular lip colors were browns and plums, particularly as the decade drew to a close. Both colors are difficult for stage use as they look dull and flat. I suggest that you choose a warmer tone and add a little browny lipstick to it.

Routine: Black, Darker Skins

Deeper skins, like that of our model, will require a stronger blusher and eyeshadow. I used a plum colored eyeshadow and reddish brown blusher.

1980s Men

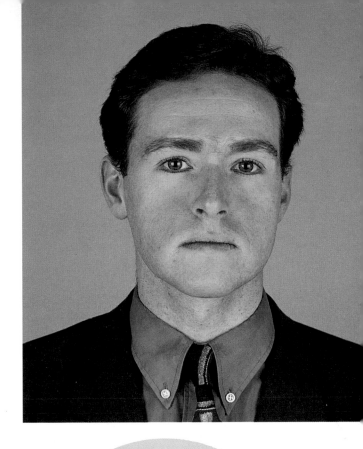

In the USA Perry Ellis, Ralph Lauren and later Calvin Klein produced elegant suits for the upwardly mobile. These "Yuppies" were very design conscious and in the UK wore Armani suits, silk shirts and ties with their carefully blown dried hairstyles. In the money conscious 1980s menswear became big business. Designers like Mugler, Comme les Garçons and later Karl Lagerfield expanded their ranges to accommodate growing male interest in clothes. Pop stars continued to influence young fashion, Boy George in female make up and long be-ribboned hair influenced other artists, and some young male fans began to use eyeliner. Bands like Spandau Ballet and Bon Jovi did set trends but the most significant trend came about when Don Johnson appeared in *Miami Vice* carefully unshaven. This "designer stubble" had a huge impact causing shaver manufacturers to introduce electric razors to give an unshaven look. In this decade hairstyles were generally casual, sometimes long and worn in a pony tail, sometimes short. Young men were becoming face conscious and began to borrow their girlfriends' moisturizers, they used shaving balms and kept their hair in place with gel. The most daring tried tinted moisturizers and had sunbed tans. Beards and moustaches were not fashionable during this period.

> *"Your image should be a positive thing that will help you to succeed, but if it becomes too much of a trademark, it can be a millstone around your neck."*
> Diane Mather, Public Image Consultancy

Keynotes

- shortish, blow-dried casual hairstyles kept in shape with gel or hairspray
- designer beard stubble

Routine

This is a basic straight make-up.

Plays, Musicals and Operas Set in Particular Periods

As this book is about period make-up I felt that it would be useful to give an idea of some well-known examples of plays, musicals and operas set in particular periods. Of course, directors may choose to set a play in another period, this often happens with Shakespeare for example. So this is just a basic list of productions and the periods they are usually set in according to the writers. Sometimes a play was written in one decade but was not staged until the following decade. Thereafter productions tend to follow the period in which the play was first performed, rather than when it was written.

EGYPTIAN

Äida, Verdi
Antony and Cleopatra, Shakespeare
Caesar and Cleopatra, George Bernard Shaw

ELIZABETHAN

The Alchemist, Ben Jonson
As You Like It, Shakespeare
Elizabeth the Queen, Maxwell Anderson
A Mad World, My Masters, Thomas Middleton
Mary Stuart, Schiller
Merry Wives of Windsor, Shakespeare
Much Ado About Nothing, Shakespeare
The Revenger's Tragedy, Anon
Twelfth Night, Shakespeare
Vivat, Vivat Regina!, Robert Bolt
Volpone, Ben Jonson

JACOBEAN

The Changeling, Thomas Middleton & William Rowley
The Duchess of Malfi, John Webster
'Tis Pity She's a Whore, John Ford
The White Devil, John Webster

THE 17TH CENTURY: RESTORATION

The Country Wife, William Wycherley
Love for Love, William Congreve
Marriage à la Mode, John Dryden
The Relapse, Sir John Vanbrugh

LATE 1800s-1910: EDWARDIAN

The Cherry Orchard, Anton Chekhov
Hedda Gabler, Henrik Ibsen
An Ideal Husband, Oscar Wilde
The Importance of Being Earnest, Oscar Wilde
An Inspector Calls, J.B. Priestley
A Little Night Music, Stephen Sondheim
Paint Your Wagon, Lerner and Loewe

1920s

The Boy Friend, Sandy Wilson
Bitter Sweet, Noël Coward
Desire under the Elms, Eugene O'Neill
Hay Fever, Noël Coward
Juno and the Paycock, Sean O'Casey
Oh, Kay, George Gershwin
Ma Rainey's Black Bottom, August Wilson
Mack and Mabel, Jerry Herman
Thark, Ben Travers

17TH CENTURY

The Misanthrope, Moilère
School for Wives, Molière
Tartuffe, Molière

18TH CENTURY

The Beggar's Opera, John Gay
Les Liaisons Dangereuses, Christopher Hampton
The Rivals, Richard Brinsley Sheridan
The School for Scandal, Richard Brinsley Sheridan

19TH CENTURY: VICTORIAN

La Bohème, Puccini
A Flea in her Ear, Georges Feydeau
The King and I, Rodgers and Hammerstein
A Month in the Country, Turganev
Patience, Gilbert and Sullivan

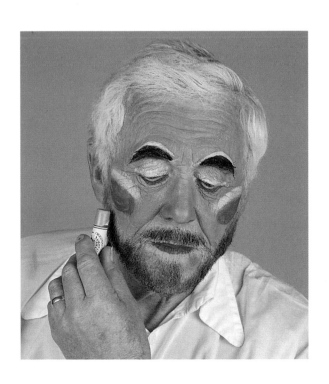

1950s

Cat on a Hot Tin Roof, Tennessee Williams
Guys and Dolls, Frank Loesser
Look Back in Anger, John Osborne
Separate Tables, Terence Rattigan
A View from the Bridge, Arthur Miller
West Side Story, Bernstein and Sondheim

1960s

The Birthday Party, Harold Pinter
Entertaining Mr Sloane, Joe Orton
Hair, Ragni, Rado and McDermot
The Odd Couple, Neil Simon
Philadelphia Here I Come!, Brian Friel
Sweet Charity, Neil Simon

1930s

Blood Wedding, Frederico Garcia Lorca
Crazy for You, George and Ira Gershwin
Golden Boy, Clifford Odets
Grand Hotel, Wright, Forrest and Yeston
The House of Barnardo Alba, Frederico
   García Lorca
Private Lives, Noël Coward
Time and the Conways, J.B. Priestley
Waiting for Lefty, Clifford Odets

1940s

Bent, Martin Sherman
Blithe Spirit, Noël Coward
City of Angels, Coleman and Zippel
Death of a Salesman, Arthur Miller
Lost in Yonkers, Neil Simon
South Pacific, Rodgers and Hammerstein
A Streetcar Named Desire, Tennessee
   Williams

1970s

Abigail's Party, Mike Leigh
American Buffalo, David Mamet
The Norman Conquests, Alan Ayckbourn
The Prisoner of Second Avenue, Neil Simon
Travesties, Tom Stoppard

1980s

Glengarry Glen Ross, David Mamet
Hapgood, Tom Stoppard
Noises Off, Michael Frayn
The Normal Heart, Larry Kramer
Sisterly Feelings, Alan Ayckbourn
Torch Song Trilogy, Harvey Fierstein

Specific Make-up Used in Photographs

I thought it would be useful for readers to know what make-up was used on the models in the photographs.

WOMEN

For all the pre-twentieth century faces I used foundations that give a sense of what they used. So that, for example, the painted ladies were all made up with Kryolan Paint stick which gives a matte covered finish. Below I have listed all the foundation and rouge colors used. The eyes were made up with cake eyeliners and the socket shadows were created with matte brown powder shadows. I used ordinary lipsticks in the appropriate colors for the mouths and theatrical eyeshadows. All the professional stage colors used were either Kryolan, Bob Kelly or Max Factor (sadly just one Factor product left).

Ancient Egyptian

Face and body – Aquacolor EK 1
Eye make-up – Aquacolor blue, green and
   black
Cheeks – Dry rouge T1
Powder – TL3 Translucent loose powder

Elizabethan

Face – white Paint stick
       white powder
Cheeks – dry rouge T1

Jacobean

Face – 1W Paint stick
Chest – 1W cake make-up
Cheeks – soft pink dry rouge
Powder – TL3 Translucent loose powder

Restoration

Face – 1W Paint stick
Chest – 1W cake make-up
Eyeshadow – blue Supracolor
Cheeks – soft pink dry rouge
Powder – TL3 Translucent loose powder

18th Century (Lady of Fashion)

Face – white Paint stick
  white powder
Chest – white cake make-up
Cheeks – dry rouge TC2

Victorian

Face – 1W Paint stick
Chest – 1W cake make-up
Cheeks – soft pink dry rouge
Powder – TL3 Translucent loose powder

Victorian/Edwardian Theatrical Make-up

Face – EF 85 Paint stick
Cheeks and other red areas – red lining color
Eyeshadow – bright light lining color
Eyebrows and eyelines – black pencil
White lines – white lining color

Edwardian

Face – 1W Paint stick
Chest – 1W cake make-up
Cheeks – R20 dry rouge
Powder – TL3 Translucent loose powder

TWENTIETH CENTURY

For these make-ups, with the exception of the 1920s, I used Kryolan face cream stick make-up, a television foundation. I used Flori Roberts foundation on the 1960s and 1980s darker skinned models. Post 1960s the eyeshadows were day make-up colors, as were most of the lipsticks.

1920s Bright Young Things

Face and Chest – 1W Aquacolor applied
  heavily
Cheeks – dry rouge T1
Eyeshadow – matte charcoal powder shadow
Lips – EF9 Supracolor
Powder – Translucent loose powder

1930s Hollywood Style

Face – 3W face cream stick
Chest – 3W cake make-up
Eyeshadow – blue Supracolor mixed with
  highlight
Cheeks – O75 dry rouge
Powder – Translucent loose powder

1930s to 1940s Theatrical Make-up

Face – 3W Paint stick
Cheeks – SM
Eyeshadow – blue lining color
Eyebrows and lines – dark brown pencil
Lips and dots – scarlet lipstick

1940s Wartime

Face – 5W face cream stick
Body – 5W cake make-up
Cheeks – cream rouge R21
Eyeshadow – powder highlighter
Powder – TL3 Translucent loose powder

1940s Hollywood Glamour

Face – 3W face cream stick
Cheeks – R20 dry rouge
Eyeshadow – blue Supracolor mixed with
    highlight
Powder – TL3 Translucent loose powder

1950s Sophistication

Face – 5W face cream stick
Chest – 5W cake make-up
Cheeks – R20 dry rouge
Eyeshadow – green Supracolor
Powder – TL3 Translucent loose powder

1950s The Sex Kitten

Face – 5W face cream stick
Eyeshadow – 1W Paint stick
Powder – TL3 Translucent loose powder

1960s Swinging London

Face – Flori Roberts Touché Satin-brown
    Satin
Eyeshadows – green Supracolor
             – white powder shadow
Cheeks – under bones – dark brown powder
    shadow — on bones – T1 dry rouge

1960s Twiggy

Face – 5W face cream stick
Body – 5W cake make-up
Eyeshadows – white cream stick plus
             – white powder shadow
Cheeks – under bones 665G dry rouge
        – on bones 075 dry rouge
Powder – TL3 Translucent loose powder

1970s High Fashion

Face – 6W face cream stick
Body – 6W cake make-up
Cheeks – soft pink dry rouge with a high-
    light shimmer added
Eyes – shimmer shadows in blue, pink and
    blue/green
Powder – TL3 Translucent loose powder

1970s Punk

Face – Television Clown White Aquacolor
Eyeshadow – matte charcoal powder shadow
Cheeks – dry rouge 665G
Mouth – EF9 Supracolor
Powder – TL3 Translucent loose powder

1980s Power Dressing

Face – 9W Aquacolor
Cheeks – Flori Roberts
Eyeshadow – Flori Roberts
Powder – TL3 Translucent loose powder

MEN

The following make-up was used for all the white male models except for the Fop and the Theatrical make-ups.

Face – cake make-up either 7 or 8W
Cheeks – TC2 dry rouge (unless stated otherwise)
Eyelines and eyebrows – cake liner or dark brown pencil
Powder – Translucent loose TL3
Highlighting eyelids – 1W Paint stick

For black models the following make-up was used.

Face – no foundation needed
Cheeks – T1 dry rouge
Eyelines and brows – black cake eyeliner
Powder – Translucent loose TL3 (trust me)
Highlighting eyelids – GG Paint stick

18th Century The Fop

Face – white Cremestick
Cheeks – T1 dry rouge
Eyeshadow – blue Supracolor mixed with the white
Eyebrows – black pencil
Powder – white

Victorian/Edwardian Theatrical Make-up

Face – EKF 7
Cheeks and other red areas – red lining color
Eyebrows – black pencil
Highlights – white lining color

1930s to 1940s Theatrical Make-up

Face – EKF 8
Cheeks – T1 dry rouge
Eyeshadow – blue lining color
Eyebrows and lines – dark brown pencil
Lips and dots – bright red lining color

Glossary

Aquacolor A creamy cake make-up which needs a slightly damp sponge to apply it. Aquacolors, as well as coming in a large range of skin tones, come in a wide range of colors including gold and silver.

Cake Make-up see pancake

Eyeline A fine line of pencil or cake eyeliner which defines the top eyelid at the edge of the eyelash roots and the bottom lid in the same way. These two lines *never* join.

Fop A fashionable man who took his clothes, make-up and hairstyles to extreme lengths. The term is mainly used in relation to Restoration times.

Highlights To pick out pale areas of the face either naturally or with the use of a very pale foundation. It also means the pale foundation you use.

Lipcolor This means lipstick or a theatrical lip rouge.

Paint The old word for foundation and rouge used from the Middle Ages to the early twentieth century. The most desirable was Venitian Ceruse, white lead mixed in Elizabethan times with vinegar and later with water or egg white. It was applied with a damp cloth or a rabbit's foot and sometimes glazed with egg white to give a sheen. Red lead paint was laid over the white to give color to the cheeks. Paint is sometimes referred to as Court Plaster.

Panstick also known as Cremestick, Face Cream Stick and Paint Stick. It is a highly pigmented cream foundation that comes in a twistup stick formula. Panstick was originally created by Max Factor. Throughout the book the term cream stick is used for this product.

Pancake The original waterbased pancake was invented by Max Factor but other companies also developed cake make-ups. Cake make-up is used with a wet sponge and is self-setting. Pancake make-up, although a Max Factor brand name, is an extensively used term in the theatre.

Patches Black shapes made from a variety of things used to cover damaged skins or as facial decorations. See page 34 for further information.

Plumpers Small cork balls worn in the mouth under the cheekbones to fill out the cavities caused by the loss of teeth.

Rouge This meant not only cheek color but lip stain as well. Wealthy Elizabethans used red of fucus, a permanent stain, which was actually deadly red mercuric sulphide. Other lip colorings over the centuries included red lead, cochineal, carmine and the Victorian rouge papers.

Shading (Shadow) Applying dark brown make-up to particular areas of the face to make them less noticeable.

Socket Shadow A dark brown make-up used to emphasize the edge of the socket bone where the top of the eyelid finishes.

Spanish Wool A pad of hair or wool impregnated with dye which was rubbed over the cheeks to color them.

Bibliography

Angeloglou, Maggie *A History of Make-up*, Studio Vista, 1970

Best, Geoffrey *Mid Victoria Britain 1851-75*, Fontane Press, 1979

Blum, Daniel *A Pictorial Guide to the Movies*, Spring Books, 1958

Burke, John *History of England*, Book Club Associates, 1978

Corson, Richard *Fashions in Make-up from Ancient to Modern Times*, Peter Owen, 1972

de Castelbajac, Kate *The Face of the Century*, Thames & Hudson

Falkus, Christopher *The Life and Times of Charles II*, Weidenfeld & Nicholson, 1972

Gernsheim, Alison *Victorian and Edwardian Fashion - A Photographic Survey*, Douer Publications Inc., 1981

Golby, J.M., Ed *Culture and Society in Britain 1850-1890*, Oxford Press, 1986

Grant, Ian & Madden, Nicholas *The Countryside at War*, Jupiter Books, 1975

Keenan, Brigid *The Women We Wanted to Look Like*, St Martins Press, 1978

Kratochirt, Laurie, Ed *Rolling Stone - the photographs*, Simon & Schuster, 1989

Laver, James *Costumer and Fashion*, Thames & Hudson, 1995

Middlemas, Keith *The Life and Times of Edward VII*, Weidenfeld & Nicholson, 1972

Palmer, Alan *The Life and Times of George IV*, Weidenfeld & Nicholson, 1972

Swinfield, Rosemarie *Stage Make-up basics for 1990s*, Rosemarie Swinfield Publications, 1989

Taylor, Derek *It was Twenty Years Ago Today* Bantam Press, 1987

Trewin, J.C., Mander, Raymond and Mitchenson, Joe *The Gay Twenties*, Macdonald & Co., 1958

Vickers, Hugo *Cecil Beaton - the authorised Biography*, Weidenfeld & Nicholson, 1985

Williams, Neville *The Life and Times of Elizabeth I*, Weidenfeld & Nicholson, 1972

More Great Books to Help Improve Your Theater Craft!

Stage Makeup Step-By-Step Bring even more realism to your stage! Color step-by-step photographic sequences guide you through stylized fantasy work, period makeup and special effects, including cuts, stitches, black eyes and bruising for theater, film and television. #70272/$23.99/128 pages/500+ color illus.

Stage Lighting Step-By-Step Create professional lighting effects with this comprehensive guide to the fundamentals of light design for all types of theater productions. You'll learn the secrets of electrical theory, rigging lights, lighting designs, and how to achieve the right atmosphere whatever your budget.
 #70365/$24.99/144 pages/250+ color illus.

Encyclopedia of Acting Techniques Perfect your performances - from drama to farce - with these professional tips and techniques for strengthening your acting skills. You'll find exercises for sharpening your focus and concentration, refining stage movement, improving voice - all illustrated with practical step-by-step reference pictures in full color. #70363/$26.99/160 pages /390 color illus.

The Stagecraft Handbook Put your set on stage quickly and inexpensively! You'll master every aspect of scenery construction as you study a wealth of drawings and photographs accompanied by tips on shop organization, tools, safety, materials, construction techniques and more! # 70311/$21.99/206 pages/244 b&w illus./paperback

Staging Musical Theatre: A Complete Guide for Directors, Choreographers and Producers Make your opening night a success using this comprehensive guide that covers everything you need to know to put a show on the boards - from selecting, analyzing and interpreting a musical to conducting productive rehearsals. #70337/$19.99/192 pages/53 b&w illus./paperback

Stage Costume Step-By-Step Create splendid theatrical costumes that evoke the grandeur of times both past and present! You'll find descriptions, measurement guidelines, cutting instructions and assembly directions for a myriad of costumes - from Tudor and Elizabethan to Puritan and contemporary dress. #70307/$21.99/144 pages/300+ color illus.

Drawing Scenery for Theater, Film and Television A strong design will "set the stage" for your production. Step-by-step directions show you how to select materials, create proper perspective, shade and tone with a variety of sketching methods. #70256/$19.99/176 pages/paperback

Stage Lighting Revealed Whether you're a novice or an experienced designer, you'll get the answers to all your lighting questions. In-depth instruction covers design, layout, equipment and lighting positions. #70201/$18.99/176 pages/paperback

The Prop Builder's Mask-Making Handbook A step-by-step guide exploring all the procedures of mask-making from choosing the material to the painting or dying of the finished product. Referenced are ten different materials and instructions on how to create character masks, leather masks, commedia del'arte and more! #70086/$19.99/204 pages/paperback

The Stage Management Handbook Uncover a wealth of helpful guidance and practical advice for performing a show - from pre-production to performance! Plus, you'll discover insights into the organizational structure of some theaters. #70102/$17.99/192 pages/57 illus./paperback

Drafting Scenery for Theater, Film and Television Drafting scenery techniques for three media are covered in depth in this first-of-its-kind book. #70039/$16.95/176 pages/124 illus./paperback

The Prop Builder's Molding & Casting Handbook Discover the first step-by-step guide to contain all the molding and casting procedures useful to every theater props builder! Includes information on the selection and use of rubber materials and procedure for making breakaway glass. #70088/$19.99/238 pages/paperback

Improvisation Starters Spark your creativity with over 900 exercises you can apply to character conflicts, solo improvisations, physical positions and more! #70058/$11.99/160 pages/paperback

The Theater Props Handbook Excellent photographs and step-by-step instructions show you the materials and techniques used to construct over 100 theater props. #70111/$19.99/288 pages/paperback

Stockists

UK

Charles H Fox Ltd
22 Tavistock Street
London WC2E 7PY

Screenface
24 Powis Terrace
London W11 1JH

USA

Kryolan Corporation
132 Ninth Street
San Francisco
California
CA 94103

Bob Kelly Cosmetics
151 West 46th Street
New York
NY 10036

Australia

Johanne Santry
7 Batemans Road
Gladsville
NSW 2111

Germany

Kryolan
Papierstraße 10
D-1000
Berlin S1

Acknowledgments

Marian Titchmarsh
Cassie
Angela Marber
Wardrobe – The Royal Academy
  of Dramatic Art
Wardrobe – LAMDA
The National Art Library,
  Victoria & Albert Museum
Terry Harris
Derek Easton – wigs
Charles H. Fox Ltd
Screenface Ltd

Marie Hood
Dolly Swinfield
Rodney Cottier
Muriel Ballingol Peattie
Wayne Gould at Interstate
Richard Morris
Alan Scott
Colin Willoughby for the photographs

All our models
and David... for being 'Supreme'

Blank Charts

We provide below a blank full face chart and
eye detail for you to photocopy. Use them to
record your own character make-up.

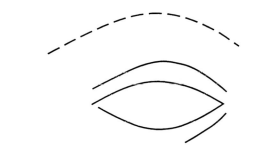

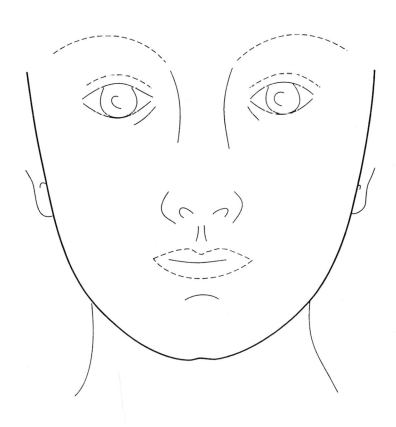

Index